MARIE JONES

Stones
in His Pocket

&

A Night
in November

NICK HERN BOOKS
London

www.nickhernbooks.co.uk

A Nick Hern Book

Stones in His Pockets first published with *A Night in November* in Great Britain in 2000 as a paperback original by Nick Hern Books Limited, 14 Larden Road, London W3 7ST

Stones in His Pockets copyright © Marie Jones 2000

A Night in November first published in 1995, copyright © Marie Jones 1995

Marie Jones has asserted her right to be identified as author of this work

Front cover image design by Scarlet

Lines on p. 25 from 'Whatever You Say, Nothing', from *Opened Ground*, by Seamus Heaney, quoted with permission from Faber and Faber Ltd and Farrar, Straus & Giroux in the USA

Typeset by Country Setting, Kingsdown, Kent CT14 8ES

Printed and bound in Great Britain by Bookmarque, Croydon, Surrey

A CIP catalogue record for this book is available from the British Library

ISBN 1 85459 494 X

STONES IN HIS POCKETS

Stones in His Pockets was first performed in Belfast at the Lyric Theatre on 3 June 1999, and was staged at the Tricycle Theatre, London, in August 1999. It opened at the New Ambassadors Theatre, London, on 24 May 2000, with the following cast:

JAKE QUINN   Sean Campion
CHARLIE CONLON   Conleth Hill

Director Ian McElhinney
Set Designer Jack Kirwan
Lighting Designer James C. McFetridge

Characters

CHARLIE CONLON, *mid thirties*

JAKE QUINN, *mid thirties*

CHARLIE *and* JAKE *play all the other characters in the play:*

SIMON, *first A.D.* (*Ambitious Dublin 4 type*)

AISLING, *third A.D., young, pretty, anxious to impress those above her, no interest in those beneath*

MICKEY, *a local in his seventies, was an extra in* The Quiet Man

CLEM, *the director, English, quiet nature, not much understanding of the local community*

SEAN, *a young local lad*

FIN, *a young local, Sean's friend*

CAROLINE GIOVANNI, *American star*

JOHN, *accent coach*

BROTHER GERARD, *local teacher*

DAVE, *a crew member, Cockney*

JOCK CAMPBELL, *Caroline's security man, Scottish*

Setting

A scenic spot near a small village in Co. Kerry

ACT ONE

CHARLIE *stands front stage as if queuing up at a catering truck.*

JAKE *is lounging in the sun.*

CHARLIE. I'll have the lemon meringue pie please . . . I know I was up before but it's not for me . . . it's for my mate . . . yes he is, he is an extra I swear . . . he can't come and get it himself because he has just sprained his ankle . . . okay . . . (*To man behind him.*) don't shuv there's plenty left . . . (*To* CATERER.) an accident report sheet? . . . he only went over on it, it's not life threatening . . . no he doesn't want a full dinner he only wants the sweet . . . (*To man behind him.*) I know we are only meant to have one helping but it's not for me . . . (*To* CATERER.) Look, I don't know why he can eat a sweet and not his dinner if he's sick, what am I a doctor or something . . . the fella asked me to go and get him a helping of lemon meringue pie . . . fine fine . . . No problem. (*Walks away.*)

Jesus Christ the Spanish Inquisition to get a bloody pudding.

JAKE. They've got wise to the extras . . . first couple of days ones were bringing their families down and feeding them too . . . (*Laughs.*) My mate has sprained his ankle . . . not very good was it . . . have you Ballycastle men no imagination . . .

CHARLIE. How do you know I am from Ballycastle?

JAKE. You were in the pub last night talking to a few of the locals . . . small town, word gets round . . . Jake Quinn . . . how are you doin' Charlie.

CHARLIE. What is this, the caterer gettin' on like he was trained by the R.U.C and you by the Special Branch . . . no fear of gettin' homesick anyway.

JAKE. How did you end up here.

CHARLIE (*furtively looks around him*). You mean you don't know . . . was there a break down in intelligence?

JAKE. You're very jumpy.

CHARLIE. Have to be man . . . I'm on the run.

SIMON. Aisling, get this lot back to work. Use a cattle prod if you have to. What about these catering vans?

AISLING. Just moving them now, Simon. Thank you. (*Gesturing to vehicles.*)

SIMON. I'm going to get Miss Giovanni from her Winnebago now.

AISLING (*third A.D.*). Quiet everyone settle . . . please finish your lunch quickly before we lose the light . . . the next shot is a close-up on reacting to you . . . then we will turn the camera and have you reacting to Maeve . . . remember what you are reacting to . . . Maeve is telling you she will plead your case to her father . . . remember your positions exactly and those of you who were wearing caps . . . please put them on.

CHARLIE (*to* JAKE). Was I wearing a cap, I can't remember.

JAKE (*smirks*). So you're on the run then.

CHARLIE. Keep your voice down.

JAKE. On the run.

CHARLIE. Aye.

JAKE. On the run from who?

CHARLIE. The Boys . . . understand.

JAKE. Jesus . . . no messin'.

CHARLIE. Aye they weren't bad though, they give me a head start . . . they says Charlie, we will close our eyes and count to twenty and you run like the hammers . . . I thought that it was very dacent.

JAKE (*to* CHARLIE). You don't have to tell me if you don't want to . . . only making conversation.

CHARLIE. Aye, sorry mate, it was the lemon meringue pie interrogation that got to me . . . well I am on the run, sort of . . . had a video shop that went bust . . . them Extra Vision bastards . . . I never heard one person in Ballycastle complain to me before them hures opened up . . . you know . . . if a video was out the customers would take something else, no problem . . . the big boys move in and gullible Charlie here thinks . . . my customers are loyal.

JAKE. Look out, here she comes . . . You were just in front of me beside oul Mickey and you had your hat on.

CHARLIE. Sure it doesn't matter.

MICKEY. Oh it will surely matter, they will check thon Polaroid and see for sure who was wearing what and you don't want to be gettin' yourself in trouble with your one with the yoke on her ear . . . you have to keep your nose clean for thon one has a gob on her that would turn milk.

CHARLIE (*puts his cap on*). Happy now, Mickey?

MICKEY. Not me fella, I'm only warning you, if you don't want to be replaced you do as you're bid . . . just say nothin' and you will be forty quid a day the wiser, that's my motto Jake.

JAKE. Aye right Mickey.

CHARLIE. Right pain in the ass.

JAKE (to CHARLIE). My mother's third cousin. Do you know that man's famous. He's the last surviving extra on *The Quiet Man* . . . but don't get him started. Where were we . . . aye the Extra Vision hures.

CHARLIE. Aye . . . I says to myself . . . they won't desert me . . . my customers won't desert me . . . I am one of them, support your own and all that . . . fuck was I wrong . . . (*Mimics them.*) Charlie you have to have more than two copies of a video, Extra Vision has loads . . . Charlie you want to see the range Extra Vision has . . . then they stopped saying anything 'cos they just stopped coming . . . so I got up one morning, . . . all my plans for the future in a heap of out-of-date movies . . . I couldn't start all over again . . . started all over again so many times I've lost count . . . this time I just couldn't do it . . . so I closed the door on the shop . . . videos still on the shelves, nothing touched . . . threw the tent in the boot and decided to do Ireland . . . what about you.

JAKE. Well I can't follow that.

CHARLIE. Ah don't mind me . . . just thought I would get it all out at once, save the locals making it up for me . . . oh and the other thing, my girlfriend dumped me too . . . talk about kicking a man when he is on the floor . . . and you'll not believe this.

JAKE. She is going out with the manager of Extra Vision.

CHARLIE. How did you know?

JAKE. You told the story last night in the pub to a second cousin of mine.

CHARLIE. Jesus, that's me and gin . . . bad combo . . . anyway, the place is coming down with Hollywood stars . . . it's a who's who of who's bonked who, and me, Charlie Conlon is a topic of conversation . . .

JAKE. We are used to that lot . . . it's outsiders coming in and taking jobs we don't like.

CHARLIE. Place is coming down with outsiders . . . it's like a bloody circus . . . there she is . . . look . . . me, Charlie Conlon only ten feet away from Caroline Giovanni . . . I'd give her one alright.

CAROLINE *and dialect coach.*

CAROLINE (*as she crosses*). Can I try the other earrings? These are too dingly, dangly. (*Practises.*) I will speak to my father, you have suffered enough.

JOHN. You're doing great Caroline . . . remember always to soften the a; and elongate it . . . I will speak to my father, you have suffered enough.

CAROLINE (*she repeats badly*). I will speak to my faaather, no . . . I will speak to my fetherr . . . shit . . .

JOHN. No Caroline put your tongue behind your teeth.

CAROLINE. Thaaather.

JOHN. No . . . No, your bottom teeth.

CAROLINE. Faaather . . . fetthe . . . fatttther . . . shit . . . these people will think it sounds ridiculous.

JOHN. Don't worry . . . Caroline . . . Ireland is only one per cent of the market.

CAROLINE. I want to get it right John.

CHARLIE (*to* JAKE). I love that, huh . . . half of America here is playing Irish people and they say I am the outsider.

JAKE. They promised the extras would be local . . . she is gorgeous.

CHARLIE. I got it fair and square . . . saw the Ad, extras wanted and they liked the look of me . . . pitched my tent and here I am . . . great money and free grub . . . it's a gift . . . Would you . . . you know, give her one?

JAKE. No chance of getting near her.

SIMON Right, let's go for this now. Good morning, Caroline, looking lovely this morning, love those earrings.

AISLING. Simon will I bring Rory out yet?

SIMON. No . . . it's bloody freezin' . . . he will go crazy hangin' about.

AISLING. Does Maeve not need to see him . . . you know the big moment of electricity.

SIMON. No . . . he comes over the hill just as she turns away from the mob. It's the next shot (*Flirting.*) silly girl.

AISLING. I'll go get his blankets . . . and have him stand by.

SIMON. Hey Aisling.

AISLING. Yes Simon.

SIMON. What do you call a Kerryman with brains?

AISLING. I don't know Simon.

SIMON. Dangerous.

They laugh.

AISLING. I don't get it Simon.

SIMON. You will Aisling, you will.

CHARLIE (*to* JAKE). What are we supposed to do?

JAKE. Look at her lookin' at us looking dispossessed.

CHARLIE. Dispo what?

JAKE. Like this. (JAKE *demonstrates.*)

SIMON. Happy to go Caroline. Turnover, Speed, mark it alright Clem, ACTION.

They look dispossessed, music plays.

SIMON. Cut . . . beautiful Caroline . . . Stay in your places 'til we check the gate. Someone get Caroline a cup of coffee.

JAKE (*to* CHARLIE). Terrible bloody accent.

CHARLIE. Doesn't matter . . . been that many film stars playing Irish leads everybody thinks that's the way we talk now . . . I have my own film here . . .

JAKE. A Film?

CHARLIE. Yeah . . . I sat in my shop day after day watching movies and I says to myself . . . Charlie, you could do that so I did . . . here it is . . . and here I am right smack in the middle of the people that can make it happen . . . I'll choose my moment and wey hey.

JAKE. I'm impressed Charlie.

CHARLIE. Don't grovel, you will have to audition like the rest.

CAROLINE. It's not right John . . . I want it to be right . . . the rhythm is wrong.

JOHN. Fine let's go to the pub the night . . . mix with the locals . . . get a feel.

CAROLINE. Yeah . . . yeah I will . . . I think I would quite like that.

JOHN. . . . but be careful Caroline, you can't be too exact, you won't get away with it in Hollywood, they won't understand.

CAROLINE. Hollywood is shit John . . . a crock of shit . . . look around this place . . . god it's just heaven on earth . . . I love this place . . . I'm third generation you know, on my mother's side . . . I do get a real feeling of belonging here you know that. You people are so simple, uncomplicated, contented.

CHARLIE (*to* JAKE). It would founder you up here. That wind would cut the arse off ye.

JAKE. Be a while yet, have to turn the camera on us.

CHARLIE. So then it's us lookin' dispossessed, luking at her with loads of land.

JAKE. Nah, it's not us they want it's the Blasket Islands.

CHARLIE (*looks around*). Bloody amazing.

JAKE. Yeah . . . they'll get a big shot of the Blaskets and the peasants, then Rory comes over the hill behind us like he is walking out of the sea. When he has his line, the lot of us disappear, even the Blasket Islands.

AISLING (*second A.D.*). Quiet everyone . . . settle . . . that's a wrap for the extras . . . we will pick this up tomorrow afternoon . . . quiet settle . . . I want all the extras in the turf-digging scene in costume by seven a.m. tomorrow morning . . . and make sure you leave all costumes in the Community centre . . . don't be tempted to go home in them . . . quiet . . . settle . . . that is all the men in scene 37 . . . tomorrow at seven a.m . . . breakfast will be from six.

CHARLIE *has his script in his hand.*

CHARLIE (*to* AISLING). Excuse me.

AISLING (*stops him with her hand as she speaks into her walkie talkie*). . . . . Hi Simon . . . Yeah Kurt is mad we're not getting to his scene . . . he was psyched up for it . . . right will do . . . cheers Simon.

CHARLIE. Excuse me . . . (*She stops him from speaking.*)

AISLING. Come back, come back, come back. Listen carefully everyone . . . slight change of plan you will be picked up at six-thirty a.m. tomorrow and taken to the location by minibus so that means everyone in costume by six . . . the minibus will leave from the community hall sharp at six-thirty . . .

CHARLIE. Excuse me.

AISLING (*sharply*). Yes.

> CHARLIE *bottles out and puts his script back in his pocket.*

CHARLIE. Are the ones in the Turf diggin' scene the same ones as the ones in the cart the day?

AISLING. Well where was the cart going?

CHARLIE (*blank . . . looks around for support . . . but no-one else seems to know*). I don't know.

AISLING. Taking the men to dig the turf . . . (*Stops him again.*) . . . Hi Simon . . . right . . . (*To* CHARLIE.) Excuse me.

She leaves.

MICKEY. Don't start gettin' yourself noticed . . . just keep your head down and go where they put you . . . that's how to survive as an extra.

CHARLIE. It's the gettin' up at the scrake Mickey is the killer.

MICKEY. Sure what would you be going to bed for if you have to be up for the scrake?

CHARLIE. Aye dead on Mickey . . .

MICKEY. And don't be going home in them boots . . . the continuity would cut the heels off you.

CHARLIE. I'll remember that Mickey.

MICKEY (*to* CHARLIE). Do you know I'm famous as I'm one of the few surviving extras on *The Quiet Man* . . . John Wayne called me by my first name . . . he would always refer to me as wee Mickey.

CHARLIE. Did you call him Duke?

MICKEY. No I did not, I give the man his place . . . I mind one day.

JAKE. Hey Mickey there's the forty quid man comin'.

MICKEY (*to* CHARLIE). I'll catch you later.

JAKE. He will spend that in the pub and by the morning he will owe twenty more and the morra night he will pay back the twenty straight off and by the end of the night the same thing . . . I don't think that man's liver could survive another movie.

SFX Interior changing room . . . showers running etc.

They start to undress and get into their day clothes during the following dialogue . . .

CHARLIE. Have you done this before?

JAKE. No but most of the town have, there was another big movie a few years back . . . the locals have got cute to it now . . . a woman that runs a guest house in the town had all her rooms full for the first time ever, a whole summer with a no-vacancies sign up, she was delighted with herself . . . this year she and her family are sleeping in a caravan at the bottom of the garden . . . she let their rooms out too . . . last time they loved the glamour and the attention with a few bob thrown in . . . this time it's the money and the money and the money . . . sad.

CHARLIE. Sad? . . . now hold on a minute . . . me going bust to Extra Vision is sad . . . somebody making twice what they made last year is not sad . . . you miffed cause you didn't get a part last time . . . not luk Irish enough.

JAKE. Nah I was in the States.

CHARLIE. What did you do there?

JAKE. This and that . . . you know bit of this bit of that . . .
worked a few bars, waited a few tables.

CHARLIE. Not make your fortune.

JAKE (*sarcastically*). No, came back here to be a film star.

CHARLIE. Tell ye what, this is the life.

JAKE. A background bog man . . . dead glamorous.

CHARLIE. You have to start somewhere, if you keep your
nose clean there could be a nice wee part in mine . . . could
you handle a sub machine gun . . . ?

JAKE *mimes sub machine gun action.*

CHARLIE. Don't call me, I'll call you.

JAKE. You haven't a hope Charlie, it's who you know in this
business, . . . that Aisling one, you know the one with
the Walkie Talkie grafted onto her ear . . . she is for the top
that one . . . Father is a director, wants to produce her own
films . . . and she will.

CHARLIE. I suppose it wouldn't even cross her mind that she
might not.

JAKE. Definitely not.

CHARLIE. She is only about twenty.

JAKE. Makes you sick.

CHARLIE. Yeah but if you've got it, doesn't matter if you're a
nobody . . . talent is talent . . . it wins through in the end.

JAKE. You don't believe that do ya . . .

CHARLIE (*sharply*). This is Charlie's day of good cheer,
nothing or nobody is going to put me in Joe Depressos.

JAKE (*taken aback*). Wouldn't dream of it . . .

CHARLIE. Jesus . . . look at that young fella, he has lost it.

JAKE. That's Young Sean Harkin, a second cousin of mine . . .
drugs . . . pain in the arse . . . I'm off to the Jacks.

SEAN. Jumped up tart . . . jumped up fucking tart . . .

CHARLIE. Hey mate, settle yourself.

SEAN. That hure, who does she think she is . . . I need a job.

CHARLIE. Well look at the state of you, this is big money, they can't take a chance on an extra messing it up.

SEAN. I was fucking born diggin' turf and that hurin' slag is tellin' me to piss off.

CHARLIE. She does have a point you know.

SEAN (*turns on him*). And who the fuck are you Mr Brown Noser.

CHARLIE. Nobody . . . just, an extra.

SEAN (*as he staggers off*). You're a nobody, just like me and she won't give me a job.

JAKE. Is he gone?

CHARLIE. Yeh. Come on Jake, I need a drink.

JAKE. Aye, with you in a minute. Hey Fin, you're his mate, can you not talk to Sean?

FIN. He came yesterday, but he was out of it and she told him to clear off. He was alright this morning and he asked me to put his name down. I told him to be here for two o'clock and he would get a start, but for fuck sake look at him.

JAKE. What's he on Fin?

FIN. Whatever he can get his hands on.

JAKE. Can ye not do something, say something . . . he is killing himself.

FIN (*exiting*). And say what, I mean what would you say Jake, don't do them nasty drugs, and get a life?

CHARLIE. Come on Jake. Are you alright?

JAKE. When he was a young buck, he used to look up to me, his Da's farm was next to ours . . . followed me every-where . . . Come on Charlie, I need that drink too.

CHARLIE. Don't let me drink gin . . .

Bar scene . . . background Country and Western music.

JAKE. Another gin there Kevin and a couple of pints . . .
business is boomin' then Kevin . . . a restaurant? . . . sure
you wouldn't get many in this town atin' out when they cud
ate in . . . of course the place will be comin' down with
tourists after this one . . .

SEAN *staggers up to* CHARLIE.

SEAN. Hey Brown Noser, have ye anything on ye . . . I can
pay.

CHARLIE. Piss off Sean.

SEAN. Please mate.

CHARLIE. I have nothin', clear off.

SEAN. Yis all think yis are movie stars, yis are nothing, I'm
Sean Harkin and I am a somebody and I fuckin' know yis
are all nothin' . . . wankers.

CHARLIE. Away home son, your Ma wants ye.

SEAN. Tossers . . . fuckin' tossers . . . full a shit.

He staggers away from him . . . CHARLIE *looks at him, for*
that brief moment . . . but doesn't want to think about it.

JAKE. How is it goin' Sean, . . . look at him, seventeen and
out of his head . . . keep thinkin' I should have a talk with
him . . . (*Distracted.*)

CHARLIE (*a bit pissed*). . . . . You know mate I was so
depressed . . . so depressed . . . I just couldn't even lift my
head . . . you know it just gets to you physically like . . .
I luked at myself in the mirror and I says . . . Charlie you
have lived on this planet for thirty-two years and what have
you to show for your existence . . .

JAKE. Maybe you should go on the pints man.

CHARLIE. Sorry mate . . . yeah stop this . . . no, this is
Charlie's day of good cheer. So, this woman in America, did
she dump ye?

JAKE. Nah she wanted to marry me . . . an ultimatum . . .
I couldn't do it . . . I could just about look after myself . . .
Me stuck there with a wife and kids to support and not a
clue about the future . . . a mate of mine went over the same
time, he's got a wife and two kids . . . he works two bars
and a late night restaurant . . . what kind of life is that . . .
so here I am on the dole and back living with the ma.

CHARLIE. Jesus look who is sitting in that corner.

JAKE. Caroline Giovanni . . . when did she come in?

CHARLIE. Mixing with the plebs . . . I tell you there is not a
man in here wouldn't give her one.

JAKE. There is not a man in here would get a look in.

CHARLIE. She might you know . . . for research purposes . . .
could be trying for a taste of the real thing.

JAKE. You've sex on the brain man.

CHARLIE. It's not my brain that's the problem . . . Jesus look
at the cut of Kevin the owner he is practically salivating.

JAKE. You know what he will do, he will get the wife to make
her a sandwich and when the restaurant opens he will have
a big plaque saying . . . Caroline Giovanni dined here . . .
I was right, there's Bridget haring off into the kitchen.

CHARLIE (*watching her go*). Go on ye girl ye.

JAKE. Jesus man look at her, she is so sexy.

CHARLIE. Bridget? . . . It's a gas . . . did you ever think you
would be sittin' in the same pub as Caroline Giovanni . . .
hey luk she is eyeing you up . . . or is it me . . . (*Moves
across the stage and realises she is still watching* JAKE.)
No, fuck, it's you . . .

JAKE (*shouts*). No, I have a pint on order thanks . . . yeah it's
great . . . that was a lovely scene today . . . very moving.

CHARLIE. Lying bastard.

JAKE. Yeah sure come on over . . . (*To* CHARLIE.) Jesus I am
made man, she wants to join me.

CHARLIE. Jesus I can feel my tongue tying itself in a knot . . . I'm away over to the riggers . . . I smell a waft of whacki backi comin' from that corner . . .

JAKE. Ah no man, don't leave me on my own.

CHARLIE. Big lad like you scared of a woman.

JAKE. She's not just a woman, she is Caroline Giovanni.

CHARLIE. Here she comes, I'm off . . . (*Stops . . . takes the script from his pocket.*) Just leave that sitting there . . . okay . . . don't be pushy just leave it where she can see it.

CAROLINE. You are in the movie then?

JAKE. Yeah . . . Jake Quinn . . . I'm just one of the crowd.

CAROLINE. I haven't seen you around.

JAKE. I was in that scene the day, you know when you talk to the peasants about asking your father to give the land back.

CAROLINE. I didn't notice anyone I was so uptight about my accent . . . was it alright?

JAKE. You would think you were born here.

CAROLINE. Are you local?

JAKE. Down the road.

CAROLINE. Your countryside is so beautiful.

JAKE. Yeah, you appreciate it more when you have been away . . . I was in the States for a couple of years.

CAROLINE (*not really interested*). Yeah, what part.

JAKE. New York . . . I travelled around as well, I went . . .

CAROLINE. You are enjoying the movie.

JAKE. Yeah it's . . . well different . . . I would like to get into movies proper like.

CAROLINE. You have a great face . . . great eyes . . . the camera would love you.

JAKE. It certainly loves you . . . your last movie was brilliant . . .

CAROLINE. This place is a bit crowded, would you like to come back to the hotel for a drink.

JAKE. I don't think I would be allowed.

CAROLINE. Who would stop you?

JAKE. Well we were warned not to bother you.

CAROLINE. No you were warned not to bother me unless I choose to be bothered and tonight I want you to come for a drink . . . (*Calls.*) Jock will you go get the car, I want to go back to the hotel . . . (*To* JAKE.) Would you like to travel with us.

JAKE. Yeah sure . . . (*Looks up.*) Ah well done Bridget . . . egg and onion.

CAROLINE. See you at the front door then.

JAKE. I think you should have your sandwich first.

CAROLINE. God no, I never eat after six o'clock.

JAKE. Could you pretend and take it with you?

CAROLINE. Why?

JAKE. Because this is a small town and I will get the blame if you don't.

CAROLINE *moves away.*

. . . would you like this?

CHARLIE (*delighted*). She gave me a sandwich.

JAKE. She is driving me to the hotel for a drink . . . I am going with her in the car.

CHARLIE. Jesus man you're made . . . did she notice the script?

JAKE. What did I tell you Charlie, it's who you know in this business.

CHARLIE. Tell her there could be a big part in it for her . . . brilliant death scene . . .

JAKE. Sorry Charlie, Every man for himself.

CHARLIE. Take it with you, just in case.

JAKE. Aye, all right. See ya.

DAVE, a Cockney, approaches CHARLIE.

DAVE. Hey Charlie, fancy a line?

CHARLIE. What?

DAVE. Fancy a line?

CHARLIE. Well I have never acted before but I'll give it a go. What do I have to say?

DAVE. Coke.

CHARLIE. COKE!!

DAVE. Jesus mate, want a loud hailer.

CHARLIE. Sorry . . . you got coke?

DAVE. Yeah.

CHARLIE. Happy days . . . fuck I love the movies.

Next morning . . . interior . . . changing room . . . CHARLIE is rushing about getting ready, hyper still from the coke the night before . . . JAKE enters relaxed . . . whistling to himself.

CHARLIE and JAKE change into costume.

CHARLIE. What happened man?

JAKE. I think she was trying to . . . you know . . . seduce me.

CHARLIE. You . . . Jesus she could have any man in the whole country . . . the world for Christ sake . . . or maybe she wanted a bit of rough . . . I know what it is . . . in the movie she bonks a peasant . . . in real life she bonks Kurt Steiner who is pretending he is Rory the peasant . . . but if it were real real life she would be bonking somebody like you, a nobody . . . well did you?

JAKE. I was surrounded by minders . . . pretending they weren't listening. But them boys have eyes and ears in their arse.

CHARLIE. And what did you say to her?

JAKE. I told her I wrote poetry . . . thought that would appeal to her . . . you know the handsome heady Irish poet.

CHARLIE. You write poems?

JAKE. No . . . but I had to think of something that would make me interesting, specially to somebody like her . . . talent is sexy if you have eff all else.

Flashback . . . romantic music . . . CAROLINE*'s bedroom.*

CAROLINE. Poetry . . . that's fascinating.

JAKE. Yeah.

CAROLINE. Are you published?

JAKE. No . . . well I don't believe in that.

CAROLINE. Really.

JAKE. That cheapens your poetry . . . makes it too accessible . . . then people interpret it and get it wrong.

CAROLINE. Would you recite one of your poems for me?

Present.

JAKE. So I picked one of Seamus Heaney's.

CHARLIE. Brilliant . . . and I bet ye she was none the wiser.

JAKE. None.

CHARLIE. Must try that.

Flashback.

JAKE. Who blowing up these sparks For their meagre heat, have missed The once-in-a-lifetime portent of the comet's pulsing rose.

CAROLINE. There is no of in the last line.

JAKE. Sorry.

CAROLINE. The once-in-a-lifetime portent, The comet's pulsing rose, there is no of . . . Seamus Heaney.

JAKE (*embarrassed*). Yeah.

CAROLINE. You underestimate me, Jake . . . I'm not just here to exploit the beauty of the land, I love it . . . I know the history and the poets.

JAKE. It always works on Irish girls . . .

CAROLINE. Maybe you should try a more obscure poet.

Present.

CHARLIE. Did you, you know . . . up in her room.

JAKE. Give her one? She is sort of untouchable . . . I mean she is Caroline Giovanni . . . so I just left, but I have been invited into her Winnebago for coffee.

CHARLIE. You be careful.

JAKE. What you mean careful?

CHARLIE. Well you don't want to be used like.

JAKE. She could use me any day.

CHARLIE. Then the press get hold of it. You know . . . Extra Gives Movie Star One in a Caravan . . . know, like your man Hugh Grant and the prostitute.

JAKE. Made her famous didn't it . . . and it's not a caravan it's a Winnebago.

CHARLIE. Oh excuse me . . . anyway, you go to the caravan and I will sneak up to the window with a Polaroid . . . Front page of *The Sun* . . . we could be fartin' through silk.

JAKE. No . . . the mother would kill me.

CHARLIE. Mine too . . . you know being brought up properly is a shaggin' handicap.

JAKE. Not knowing what you are going to do for the rest of your life is a bigger one.

CHARLIE. Come on man, we are on a movie . . . guys would give their left testicle to be where we are . . . forty quid a day, rubbing shoulders with stars.

JAKE. And then what, when it's over, then what?

CHARLIE. Don't even think about it, we have three weeks left . . . tell you what, the riggers are boys to hang out with . . . comin' down with coke . . . Jesus that stuff is magic I was out of my head last night . . . great job that . . . good money, all the coke you can sniff . . . what a life . . . did she get a wee chance to have a wee butchers at my script?

JAKE *brings it out of his pocket . . . obviously had forgotten.*

JAKE. Sorry Charlie, just didn't find the right moment.

CHARLIE (*disappointed*). Aye . . . these things have to be timed right . . . it's all in the timing . . . thanks anyway.

AISLING. Quiet everyone . . . settle . . . as soon as you get dressed, please make your way to the minibus immediately where Costume can check you.

CHARLIE (*eager to please*). Right dead on Aisling . . . no problem . . . we are ready . . . I will gee up the rest for you . . . and if you have a wee minute maybe you could have a wee skiff over this . . . I would love you to be involved in it . . .

AISLING (*impatiently*). What?

CHARLIE. My film.

AISLING. Post it to the Production Office . . . come on . . . get a move on.

JAKE. You are pissin' against the wind Charlie.

CHARLIE. No . . . just not quite getting the right moment.

On the bus.

CHARLIE. I haven't dug turf since I was a wee buck.

JAKE (*sarcastically*). Yeah it will be a nice romantic rural Irish scene.

CHARLIE. Ack I think it is . . . all us diggin' away at the turf . . . Maeve comin' by on her horse and clockin' Rory and him clockin' her and thinkin' . . . wow I'd love to give her one . . . and all the time the fiddles playing in the background . . . I love the movies. Unreal man.

Bus stops.

SIMON. Is there a Jake Quinn here?

JAKE. Yeah.

SIMON (*on walkie talkie to* AISLING). Aisling. Clem's not happy with the cows. The cows. He says they're not Irish enough. I don't know. Black fluffy ones, I suppose. Simon, 1st A.D. Quick word.

JAKE. Sure.

SIMON. Caroline Giovanni wants you to have coffee with her . . . The director has said you can have ten minutes . . . then you will excuse yourself and leave.

JAKE. What if she doesn't want me to leave?

SIMON. Look mate, I am telling you, you have ten minutes, and if you are not out in ten minutes I will come and get you.

CHARLIE (*to* JAKE). Jesus, ten minutes. Ten minutes . . . sure that's more than any of the rest of us would get in a lifetime.

JAKE. Jesus here's the heavy.

JOCK (*big Scottish heavy*). You Jake?

JAKE. Aye if you're Tarzan.

JOCK (*not amused*). The name is Jock Campbell . . . Ms Giovanni's security . . . You might have seen me last night in the hotel.

JAKE. No can't say I did.

JOCK. You will have ten minutes . . . I will be outside the door and when you hear me give two raps you will come out . . . I mean ten minutes and not a second more. Wait here!

JAKE. Hold on I didn't ask for this.

CHARLIE. Jesus, a brick shithouse on legs you boyo.

JAKE. Suddenly I am being treated like I'm a potential attacker . . .

CHARLIE. Now see it from their point of view . . . you are a nobody . . . that is a potential security risk, you are an Irish nobody, that is a definite security risk, you are from the arse hole of nowhere in Ireland and you could be I.R.A., major megga security risk.

JAKE. Out to kidnap her.

CHARLIE. Got it in one.

JOCK. Mr Quinn. We have you listed as Ninth Avenue, New York.

JAKE. I am not long back, I haven't changed it yet . . . you see I live here with my mother.

JOCK. When did you arrive back?

JAKE. Couple of weeks ago.

JOCK. And why did you leave America?

JAKE. I was homesick.

JOCK. And what is your mother's address?

JAKE. Listen mate, do me a favour will you . . . go and tell Miss Giovanni, thank you but no thank you . . . tell her I don't like coffee and I hope she is not too offended.

JOCK. You want me to tell her that? You're lucky to get a second chance Mr Seamus Heaney.

CHARLIE. Jesus . . . who do these people think they effen' well are?

JAKE. Me and my fekking poetry.

CHARLIE. What do you mean?

JAKE. I lied . . . she knew it was Heaney.

CHARLIE. If I had bin you I would have lied to me too . . . well nobody wants to admit to being a dickhead.

SIMON. Jake could I have a quiet word?

JAKE. What Simon . . . alright.

SIMON. I am going to get into terrible trouble if you don't keep that appointment . . . the security check is necessary . . . Ms Giovanni is worth at least six million and if anything were to happen to her . . .

JAKE. Fine, I understand that, just tell her I would not like to put her at risk.

SIMON. Jake . . . it is very important for us to keep the stars happy, she simply requested that she would like you to join her . . . and if you are clean then you should not worry about the security check.

JAKE. I had a parking fine in 1987 I think I would be a high risk . . . and what is more I object to you lot checkin' me out, this is an infringement of my privacy.

SIMON. Well if you must go chatting up important people that's the price you pay.

JAKE. Fuck it, she chatted me up.

SIMON. Look mate, don't go thinking you're anything special. Miss Giovanni has a habit of going ethnic. Helps her get into the part. I am giving you a quiet word of warning . . . Ms Giovanni does not like to be snubbed, particularly by an extra, and it might be her request that you be removed from the set, so for your own good . . .

JAKE. That's it Charlie, I am not going . . . no way, they can sack me if they like.

CHARLIE. Don't worry, just go and pass yourself . . . let her do all the talking.

JAKE. Look at all the extras, not one of them has tuk their eyes off me. Just watching and waiting.

CHARLIE. Just jealous. Forty pound a day mate, forty pound a day and another three weeks and you never know, she could be your key into the movies.

JOCK. Right, are you coming? You have ten minutes.

CHARLIE. Good luck Jake . . . (*Looks round.*)What are youse all lookin' at, he is only away to give her one, two consenting adults aren't they . . . (*To* CATERER.) I'll take Jake Quinn's baked Alaska . . . because he is having coffee with Caroline . . . yeah, well me and him and Caroline is sort of friends now . . . yes fresh cream on both would be lovely . . . no thanks two helpings is enough . . .

CAROLINE *is discovered in a yoga position centre stage, playing appropriate music.*

CAROLINE. Hi, how are you?

JAKE. Fine.

CAROLINE. Coffee?

JAKE. Yes, please.

CAROLINE. Sugar?

JAKE. Two please.

CAROLINE. Cream?

JAKE. Yes please.

JAKE. I am only allowed ten minutes.

CAROLINE. We have all the time in the world. Your accent is so beautiful . . . do you mind if you could read my lines and I put a tape on.

JAKE. I thought you had one of them professional accent people.

CAROLINE. I have but there is nothing like the real thing . . . and besides you're far better looking . . .

JAKE. Am . . . how would I go about gettin' into the movies, what is the first step?

CAROLINE (*mimics his accent*). How would I go about getting into the movies . . . that's just so beautiful . . . how do I sound?

JAKE. Sounds great.

CAROLINE. Let's start on page seven.

JAKE. How did you get started?

CAROLINE. You don't want to hear about that. This first speech.

JAKE. I mean should I have an agent or something.

CAROLINE (*angry*). You don't want to get into the movies, it's shit, real shit . . . now could you just read this for me.

JAKE. Rory will your people ever accept me . . .

CAROLINE. Don't mumble . . . I need you to articulate . . . again . . .

JAKE. But Maeve is one of the landed gentry, she wouldn't talk like us anyway.

CAROLINE (*annoyed*). Excuse me?

JAKE. She'd have been educated in England. She'd talk different like.

CAROLINE. No, but she wants to fit in. She always has.

JAKE. Ah yeh, but she wouldn't have mixed with the locals until she started going out with Rory. You wouldn't pick up an accent that quickly.

CAROLINE. Look I don't have time to sit here with you and discuss what my character would and would not do. Can we just read the script?

JAKE. No . . . I think I had better be going . . .

CAROLINE. Your time isn't up yet.

JAKE. I'm sorry. I think it is.

JAKE *makes to leave* . . . CAROLINE *shouts before he can get out.*

CAROLINE. Jock . . . I'm finished with Mr Quinn.

CAROLINE *attempts to say the words.*

CAROLINE. Rory will your people ever accept . . . no . . . shit . . . Rory . . . Rory . . . fuck. (*Screams.*) Jock get John in here now.

JAKE (*to* CHARLIE). I feel like shit man, you know, being used like that.

CHARLIE. So you were just a sex object with an accent. I did that to a girl once . . . met her on a ferry, French she was . . .

JAKE. She said the movies are shit.

CHARLIE. She gets six mill a picture and she thinks it shit, I am gettin' forty smackaronies and I think it's class.

AISLING. Quiet . . . settle . . . when Maeve approaches on the horse, everyone stops digging and looks at her . . .

CHARLIE (*excited*). Oh good Caroline Giovanni is in our scene.

AISLING. We won't have Maeve in the scene, so the top of my hand will be your eye line . . . so when the camera rolls dig until I raise my hand and my hand will be Maeve approaching on the horse . . . then you will all look up and stare at her . . . when I drop my hand you will look to the left and see Rory approaching Maeve on the horse.

CHARLIE. Oh brilliant, Kurt Steiner is gonna be in it.

AISLING. . . . Now Rory won't be in the scene.

CHARLIE (*quietly*). Fuck sake is anybody working round here, only us.

AISLING. So when you look to the left, Simon's hand will be Rory approaching Maeve on the horse. All right, everyone OK?

CHARLIE. So it us lookin' dispossessed at her hand, pretending it's Maeve on a horse lookin' sorry for us . . . I'm gonna miss all this.

JAKE. What will you do?

CHARLIE (*brings his script out*). Maybe somebody will read this and say . . . Jesus this is brilliant . . . and I tell ye man . . . I will be made . . .

JAKE. Grow up Charlie.

CHARLIE. And what, just keep touring round Ireland waiting for movies?

JAKE. Even that's dying out . . . they have used up most of the forty shades of green by now.

SIMON. Now remember . . . it's dig . . . Hands over here . . . stop . . . my hands over there . . . turn over, speed, make it . . . ready Clem . . . and action.

Music.

They dig . . . stop . . . look up . . . moving their heads as if watching galloping horses and then stop . . . then look the other way doing the same action . . .

JAKE *starts to laugh . . . then can't control himself.*

SIMON. Cut . . . yes and what is so funny mate?

JAKE. Sorry . . . it's just hard . . . you know her hand being Maeve on a horse and your hand being Rory and . . . (*Laughs.*) sorry.

SIMON. Time is fucking money here mate.

JAKE. Wasn't just me, everybody laughed.

SIMON. Right . . . quiet, we are going to go for this again . . . this time with a bit of feeling. (*Under his breath.*) Bloody extras.

They repeat the action as before . . . JAKE and CHARLIE just about control the laughter.

SIMON. And cut . . . stay in position until we check the gate.

CHARLIE. Hey Jake . . . if you were a movie star, I could be your minder . . . personal manager, line up the women, try them out first so you won't be disappointed, know like the queen has somebody to taste her dinner.

JAKE. What is the commotion over there?

CHARLIE. Where?

JAKE. Fin looks like he's in a terrible state . . . that's his Da with him . . . must be trouble . . . Fin . . . what's the trouble?

FIN. M'Da has brought terrible news Jake . . . Sean Harkin . . .
drowned himself this morning. Da says Danny Mackin was
up in his top field and saw Sean walk into the water . . .
he didn't know if he was coddin' or what for he had all
his clothes on. Danny shouted at him and said he saw Sean
comin' back out . . . Danny didn't know what to make of
it . . . then he saw him walk into the water again and never
rise out of it . . . Danny was too far away to do anything but
raise the guards . . . when the divers found him . . . his
pockets were full of stones . . . he came out of the water to
fill his pockets full of stones.

SIMON. And the gate is clear. Let's move on.

End of Act One.

ACT TWO

JAKE *enters . . . he is solemn . . . he stands for a second or two before* CHARLIE *enters . . .* CHARLIE *enters reading his script . . . He sees* JAKE, *he walks up to him and touches his arm as if to say he understands.*

AISLING. Quiet everyone . . . settle . . . On Action I want you all to cheer Rory as he emerges from the Big House . . . this is very important . . . It is the final scene where Rory is now the owner of the Big House . . . because he has married Maeve and you know he is going to hand back the land to the people. Big smiling faces and real joy . . . remember it's the big Happy Ending. Over to you Simon. Turn over.

SIMON. Cheers Aisling, Turn over, Speed, mark it and ACTION.

AISLING. Action.

SFX Music . . . they run forward . . . stop and make weak attempts at the cheer.

SIMON. Cut . . . Right everybody we are going to go for that take yet again. So . . . Rory has just married Maeve, you know now that he has inherited the land . . . come on for Christ sake show a bit more jubilation . . . You see Rory coming out of the big house, he's now the owner of the big house. You all see him and cheer. (*They cheer.*) Aisling let's show them what they're doing. PLAYBACK!

The music is played back . . . AISLING *and* SIMON *demonstrate how it should be done.*

SIMON. Come on if we don't get this we will have cloud cover. Turnover, speed, mark it and ACTION. Don't. (*To* AISLING, *who is about to say 'Action'.*)

They cheer . . . again weakly.

SIMON. Cut, Jesus!

CHARLIE. Hard work this morning. C'mon man, snap out of it.

JAKE. Are you alright, Fin.

FIN *is discovered downstage right..*

FIN. Sean always talked about getting out. He hated this place.
He used to say to me, you and me, Fin, we'll escape.
He always used that word – escape. He wanted to go to
America. He wanted to be someone. You know that last film
was made here, we were only kids, we all got carried away.
Sean used to sit watching them day after day.

SEAN (*twelve years*). Be brilliant to be in that film wouldn't it
Fin.

FIN (*twelve years*). You make loads of money.

SEAN. Will we ask can we be in it . . .

FIN. We would have to dress up in them stupid clothes, I
wouldn't be seen dead.

SEAN. But maybe they would spot us and . . . you know take
us off to America to make our own film . . . you know like
McCauley what's his name.

FIN. My Da wouldn't let me go.

SEAN. To be a millionaire?

FIN. No, sure I have to take over the shop.

SEAN. You would rather be a butcher than a millionaire?

FIN. Well no, but my Da . . .

SEAN. Cuttin' up dead meat when you could be a superstar.

FIN. I'll think about it . . . I would have to ask my Da first.

SEAN. I don't, my Da says us boys has to find something to
do 'cos well there will be no need for too many farmers . . .
hey, where will you get meat if there will be no cows soon?

FIN. No cows . . . don't talk daft . . . where will they all go?

SEAN. I don't know, America . . . all them trucks and caravans
and people, the town is going to be dead soon, we have to
get into that film.

FIN. My Da won't let me . . . he says the people's heads is gettin' carried away.

SEAN. Your Da is talking bollicks . . . they are paying thirty quid a day . . . I am going to save mine for America.

Present.

JAKE. Maybe he looked at me and realised there was no American Dream.

CHARLIE. Come on, some guys make it . . . yer man that owns the hotel, didn't he leave with fifty dollars, then comes back and buys it inside two years.

JAKE. Yeah for every one of him there is fifty who come back without an arse in their trousers.

CLEM, *the Director.*

CLEM. Hi I'm Clem Curtis the Director . . . we are goin' to have to go for another take on this . . . this scene is very important . . . this is the final scene in the movie, so let me explain . . . I know we are shooting out of sequence and I am aware that not many of you don't know the story. Hello, hello. (*To JAKE, who's not concentrating.*) . . . So I want you to imagine that when Rory walks out of that house he is about to answer all your hopes and dreams, whatever they are . . . Rory has the answer, so that is what we want to see on your faces . . . we will be doing some close-ups, so we want to see real fucking ecstasy here.

JAKE. Real fucking ecstasy? Young Sean Harkin has killed himself yesterday because of real fucking ecstasy.

CLEM. Take it easy.

JAKE. Sorry . . . it's just . . . I'm sure you understand that we are finding it hard to jump for joy.

CLEM. Yes we are aware of that and we are very sorry but we must get this shot right . . . and I am sorry for the unfortunate use of the word . . . so if you could give me some joyful animations.

SIMON. Too late Clem, those clouds are about to hit in five seconds. I think they are here for the rest of the morning . . .

shall I break the extras for an hour and go for an interior . . .
Aisling . . . break the extras.

AISLING. Okay everybody we will pick this shot up again in a
hour, so please no-one leave the set . . . At the end of the
day I want everyone to go now to costume. It's the big
celebration tomorrow in the grounds of the Big House . . .
and you will have new costumes so please see wardrobe
before you leave.

CHARLIE. Jesus, is it not the funeral the morra Jake?

JAKE. They will have to work round us . . . the whole town
will be there.

CHARLIE. Even so, they should stop anyway, mark of respect.

JAKE. It's the least they could do.

CLEM. Right folks we are in total sympathy with you all and
we have sent condolences to the family. (*Aside.*) Have we
sent condolences? . . . But I am sure you appreciate we have
been held up quite a bit with the weather. I am sorry it will
be impossible to let you all free for the funeral tomorrow . . .
we have a long day with most of you in shot from early
morning . . .

MICKEY. We have to pay our last respects . . . he was related
to most of us.

CLEM. Tomorrow is a big day for us . . . we have a marquee
being transported, truck loads of fresh flowers shipped over
from Holland, three catering companies for the wedding
feast . . . we must finish by dusk tomorrow.

MICKEY. You will have to stop for the funeral . . . we will all
be there.

CHARLIE (*to* JAKE). Excuse me interrupting you Clem, but
why don't you just go ahead and do the wedding, only most
of the guests leave to go to a funeral in the town. It's only a
story . . . this is the movies, can't you do what you want?

CLEM. We are behind schedule, if we don't do the wedding
tomorrow and get finished we are fucked.

JAKE. That's life.

CLEM. Do you people realise that each day we film it costs at least a quarter of a million dollars?

MICKEY. Then how come we only get forty pound a day?

CLEM. Jesus.

JAKE. Well said Mickey.

SIMON. Clem let me deal with it.

CLEM. They are all yours Simon . . . just don't come back with a no or the producers are goin' to have my balls.

SIMON. Listen, guys, we are in total sympathy with you . . . but if we cut filming by two hours we would be in real crisis . . . we need that for weather cover. It would be a disaster if we didn't wrap up that scene tomorrow . . . We would have to go into another hire situation for the marquees . . . the producers won't cover us if we run over . . . I am prepared to pay all of you an extra twenty quid.

MICKEY. How much did he say Jake?

JAKE. Not enough Mickey.

SIMON. . . . Guys . . . seriously . . . listen . . . Push comes to shove, we could sack all of you. Remember that.

MICKEY. He can't sack us, we are in the can.

CHARLIE. What's that Mickey?

MICKEY. We're on tape . . . in the camera . . . are you thick . . . it will luk bloody daft in the last scene if the whole lot of us luked like a whole load of other ones wouldn't it. We're in the can, in the camera, on tape – are you thick? . . . The producer may be after his balls, but it's us that has them.

CHARLIE. Jake where are you going . . . we are not allowed to leave the set.

JAKE. We have an hour, I have to go somewhere.

SFX . . . Classroom bell.

JAKE. Brother Gerard . . . Hello, Jake Quinn.

BROTHER GERARD. Jake Quinn, sure I remember you
well . . . how was America?

JAKE. Fine . . . Brother I want to talk to you about young Sean
Harkin.

BROTHER GERARD. A terrible tragedy, terrible for the
whole family. He was a grand youngin. I remember his first
year.

Flashback.

BROTHER GERARD. Cunas, cunas. Sean Harkin come up to
the front of the class please. Now Sean here is going to read
out his essay on cows . . . come on Sean.

SEAN (*eight years*). Cows are great big useful beasts. They are
more useful than humans. They are more useful because
you can get meat from them, then you can get milk and
butter and they even make good school bags. Cows are the
business because many people live off cows and they give
you no bother as long as you feed them and milk them.
A cow is even useful when it goes to the toilet because
we need the manure to fertilise the land. If I were a cow
I would feel very useful. I would rather be a dairy cow so
that I didn't have to be killed. When I grow up I am going
to have the best herd in Kerry.

Present.

BROTHER GERARD. Muy hu agus sigi sios. He was a nice
child from a good family, then he just got carried away. The
father sold off a lot of the land to make ends meet and the
kid's hopes went with it. And how are you, Jake – what has
brought you back from America?

JAKE. Homesick brother . . . am Sean, was he a kid that got
depressed or anything?

BROTHER GERARD. Not a bit of him . . . you couldn't cut
him with a bread knife . . . he lived in another world . . . a
world he lived out in his head . . . you know imagination
can be a damned curse in this country.

JAKE. What did he talk about, what did he want?

BROTHER GERARD. Tell you the truth he was as normal as the rest when it came to that . . . they wanted to be rock stars, film stars, footballers . . . if one of them had said a teacher or a dentist or something I would have dropped dead with the shock . . . problem with Sean was, he was convinced he could be all the things he wanted . . . and at times thought he was.

SFX . . . School Bell.

JAKE. Thanks Brother Gerard . . . thanks.

CHARLIE. Hurry up Jake earache was lukin' ye, I said you were at the Jacks.

JAKE. Thanks Charlie, where was I?

CHARLIE. You were standin' here.

SIMON. Aisling, change of plan. Light's perfect for the eviction scene.

AISLING. Great Simon. The natives are a bit restless, I think we should go for it quickly.

SIMON (*speaks into his walkie talkie*). Good girl. Right . . . fine Clem . . . I'll tell them . . . Quiet . . . Ms Giovanni would like to talk to you all for a moment, so don't leave your positions until she comes.

JAKE. Do we get on our knees.

CHARLIE. Give it a rest.

CAROLINE. Look, I am really sorry about what has happened . . . I know you are a small neighbourhood and everyone is greatly affected by it . . . it's such a terrible tragedy . . . I just want you all to know that I appreciate you all being here and carrying on under such sad circumstances . . . thank you . . . and well . . . just thank you.

CHARLIE *claps and encourages others.*

CHARLIE. Now that was very nice of her, she didn't have to do that.

JAKE. Know what gets me Charlie . . . these people think that it has nothing to do with them.

CHARLIE. It hasn't.

JAKE. Of course it has, terrible tragedy, I'll tell you what's a terrible tragedy, filling young Sean's head with dreams.

CHARLIE. No different from me that kid . . . like all of us . . . like you, don't *we* dream, do you not fantasise about being the cock of the walk, the boy in the big picture . . . like, why couldn't it happen to us if it happens to other people . . . eh? Do you never get carried away into that other world . . . we are no different.

JAKE. Except that we are still alive.

AISLING. Quiet everyone, settle . . . when you are ready we will do the eviction scene . . . that is, Rory and his family being evicted . . . The bailiffs gallop on, they dismount, go into the house. They eject the furniture first and then the people . . . No no. It is a silent scene . . . no angry abuse . . . you are defeated men . . . so watch in silence.

JAKE (*to* CHARLIE). Aye dead on . . . did you ever, as if all us would stand by and watch a whole family being evicted without opening our mouths . . . even if it was just . . . go on you rotten bastards, just something. Defeated broken men . . .

JAKE. Oh that's no problem . . . Typecast.

CHARLIE (*to* JAKE). Not yet . . . (*Brings the script out of his pocket.*) If only I could get one person to read this. You know they tell the rest . . . and it snowballs. That's how it happened.

JAKE. Charlie you know as well as I do if that script ever gets into one of their hands it will hit the bottom of a waste basket and never see the light of day again.

CHARLIE. Look I don't need this kind of negative shit, do ya hear.

JAKE. Then get real . . . Charlie . . .

CHARLIE. Excuse me . . . this is real . . .

JAKE. And what if they say you have written a load a bollicks and you'll never make nothing writing shit like that . . . then what?

CHARLIE. I won't believe them.

JAKE. You will Charlie, and you know it.

SIMON. OK. We're going to go for this now. Remember you're defeated, broken men. Turnover, Speed, mark it, and ACTION. OK Clem.

They enact eviction as detailed by AISLING.

Lovely . . . and we will check the gate . . . if the gate is clear that is a wrap . . . do you hear . . . quiet . . . that is a wrap for the night . . . check your calls for the morning . . . goodnight and pray for sun tomorrow or we are all in big trouble.

They take their extra clothes off.

MICKEY. That Simon fella's off his head, rain hail snow, we still get our forty quid.

CHARLIE. What about the funeral? Are they stopping to let us go to the funeral?

MICKEY. No choice we put our futs down . . . power to the people eh Jake . . . they say they will get it all done only if we have sunshine for eight hours . . . I puts my hand up like this to the wind, you see? . . . and then I gets down on the ground and I listens to the earth and then I tuk my hat off and threw it up to see what way it would land and it landed the right way up, so I says . . . it will be a scorcher, you won't see a cloud next or near the place . . . and that convinced him.

CHARLIE. That's amazing.

MICKEY. A pity it's a load of bollicks . . . here's the forty quid man comin', now that is what I call a ray of sunshine, Dermot.

They change into clothes.

JAKE. See you, Mickey. See you later. Charlie, I will take you to Sean's wake the night.

CHARLIE. But I never knew him.

JAKE. Won't matter . . . you're with me . . . hey I'm sorry for earlier.

CHARLIE. It's alright . . . I understand . . .

JAKE. I shouldn't get on to you . . . at least you're trying to do somethin' with your script . . . Mickey has watched his whole way of life fall apart around him . . . and now all it's worth is a backdrop for an American movie . . . he depends on their forty quid a day and then he lives in hope for the next one . . . he's some boy, he never lets it get to him.

LX . . . change.

JAKE. Mr Harkin . . . sorry for your trouble . . . Charlie Conlon, he's on the film.

MR HARKIN. Hello Charlie . . .

JAKE. Terrible tragedy, Mr Harkin.

MR HARKIN. Aye . . . go on in there Jake. I'll see you after the milkin' . . . rain hail or death the cows haft to be milked . . .

JAKE. Sure, I'll do that for you.

MR HARKIN. No, you're all right Jake, all Sean ever knew as a young one was the land . . . same as you Jake, aah he looked up to you . . . I didn't know what to say to him when the land had let him down . . . anyway, go on into the house, there is a feed and a bit of music . . . I can give Sean nothin' more now but a dacent wake . . . I will see you after milkin'.

The Wake.

CHARLIE *and* JAKE *as if in a room full of people . . . SFX traditional music.*

CHARLIE. Sorry for your trouble. I'm Charlie Conlon – a friend of Jake's.

JAKE. How's it goin' Malachy? . . . alright Mary? How ya Fin?

CHARLIE. How are you doin' . . . hello . . . it's like being on the set . . . the same people.

JAKE. Hello Paddy . . . Aye it's tough being in the movies.

CHARLIE. Great music.

JAKE. The family are all traditional players.

MICKEY. He is gettin' a great send off . . . some of the best players in Ireland.

JAKE. Do you not play yourself then Mickey?

MICKEY. I will get a few more gargles in me and I will see if the oul squeeze box will loosen up.

JAKE. How's it's goin' Fin? . . .

Takes FIN *aside.*

FIN. Jake, everything he wanted was somewhere else . . . he hated this town. He said it let him down . . . everybody let him down . . . but sure that couldn't be helped . . . that's the way it was and nobody's fault . . . you know some of us just accepted that life wasn't great, but he wouldn't . . . he stopped going out he just got his gear and stayed in his room with his movies . . . virtual reality. That kept him going, drugs and movies.

JAKE. What was it about that day? Why was it different from any other?

FIN. He had tried to get on the movie the day before but he was out of his head . . . Then, that night in the pub . . . they were all there . . . all arse lickin' the yanks it seemed he was right in the middle of the world he fantasised about . . . you know, the beautiful American star, the movies. He knew the crew had coke . . . they were all laughin' and joking and he just watched them and then he tried to score. He saw your woman talking to you and then he went up to her . . .

Flashback.

SEAN *staggers over to* CAROLINE.

SEAN. Caroline . . . you are Caroline Giovanni.

CAROLINE (*panics*). Go away.

SEAN. I only want to say hello, I am Sean Harkin.

CAROLINE. Get away from me.

SEAN. I won't touch you I just want to look at you.

CAROLINE. Jock . . . Jock . . . I am being pestered, get rid
of him.

JOCK (*grabs him*). Right you out, if I see you back in here
I will break your two fuking legs.

Present.

FIN. He was put out on the street, out of the pub in his own
town . . . he sat outside on the street, I went with him.

JAKE. And then he watched me go off with her didn't he?

FIN. Yeah.

JAKE. And what did he say?

FIN. Nothing.

JAKE. What did he say . . . tell me?

FIN. I said he didn't say anything.

JAKE. He must have said something.

FIN. Waster . . . fukin' waster Fin . . . what is she doing with a
waster like Jake Quinn . . . that's what he said.

JAKE. Jesus, Charlie.

CHARLIE. It's not your fault . . . not one person is to blame.

JAKE. . . . . I have to get out of here . . .

SIMON *is about to have a nervous breakdown* . . .

SIMON (*on walkie talkie*). I don't fuckin' believe this . . . two
truck loads of flowers and we have to scrap them . . . can
he not take shaggin' pills like anybody else . . . Jesus . . .
right . . . right . . . Aisling . . . Aisling.

AISLING. Aisling here Simon.

SIMON. Aisling we are going for an exterior . . . Kurt has hay fever and wants the flowers scrapped from the marquee . . . Jesus . . . two effing trucks of effing flowers.

AISLING. Oh no . . . can we send them back?

SIMON. Yeah, they'll be dead by the time they hit Holland. This is a nightmare, it took four hours to put them in for that wanker to tell us he had shaggin' hay fever TURN THAT MUSIC OFF . . . set up for the exterior street dance.

AISLING. Copy that Simon.

JAKE. Hey fella, if you have flowers now they won't go to waste, young Sean Harkin's funeral today.

SIMON. It's not up to me . . . and I can tell you by the time they get through to America and get a producer to ask another producer to ask the executive producer the young fella will be dead and buried a week and we will have a shit load of dead flowers to dump . . . Jesus I am crackin' up.

CAROLINE. Excuse me Simon . . . Jake that is very touching and of course the flowers will be delivered to the Chapel . . . Simon see to it immediately. Whatever the cost I will attend to it.

JAKE (*sourly*). Thanks.

CAROLINE. I am really sorry, it must be so hard for you.

JAKE. Yes it is . . . very hard . . . and more so when I think of the way I treated him, the way you and everybody else treated him like he was a piece of muck on their boots.

CAROLINE. Excuse me? . . . I didn't even know him.

JAKE. No, but you had him thrown out of the pub, in his own town in front of his own people, think about that for humiliation . . . think about what that did to his self esteem.

CAROLINE. I don't know what you're talking about.

JAKE. Course you don't, you come here and use us, use the place and then clear off and think about nothing you leave behind.

CAROLINE. Listen here, I work hard in this industry, I have
    worked for everything I have ever done, I have used nobody.

JAKE. Yeah well maybe this industry that you work so hard for
    might be one of the things that drove that kid to do what he
    did.

CAROLINE. Don't be ridiculous.

JAKE. You're right, I am being called now to dance up and
    down the street for the big happy ending. Yes I feel
    ridiculous.

    He walks away . . . CAROLINE *stands a moment . . . then
    leaves.*

    Music. CHARLIE *and* JAKE *dance as if with other people.*

SIMON. Cut . . . beautiful . . . the Irish know one thing, it's
    how to dance.

CHARLIE. You would think he wasn't Irish.

JAKE. He just wishes he wasn't.

SIMON. Yeah mate you're right, because every time you fuck
    up I get it in the ear from these people . . . ever hear the
    phrase . . . Irish what do you expect . . . well unfortunately
    for me they tend to include the whole nation . . . (*To his
    walkie talkie.*) Aisling break the extras for the funeral . . .
    they have an hour and a half . . . tell them anybody that
    comes back smelling of alcohol will be put off the set.

MICKEY. Holy mother a Jasis, a funeral without a drink . . .
    never heard of it happening in my life and I have bin to
    more funerals than the undertaker himself . . . a dry funeral
    in Kerry, what is happening to the world?

    JAKE *and* CHARLIE *stand face front as if in the Chapel.*
    CHARLIE *is sneezing.*

    SFX organ music.

CHARLIE. Bloody flowers . . . I suppose it doesn't matter
    about my hayfever does it . . .

JAKE. How can she do that . . . she let them walk her up to the front pew . . . she didn't even know him . . . she had him thrown out of the pub like a piece of dirt . . . bitch.

CHARLIE. She paid for the flowers that's why . . . Anyway it's nice for the family . . . come on settle yourself, don't blame her . . . she didn't know the kid was going to kill himself.

JAKE. . . . I am so fucking . . .

CHARLIE. Stop it.

JAKE. Just don't know what to do . . . it's not with her, not with anybody on the film. it's . . .

CHARLIE (*sneezes*). Do you mind, but I am moving to another pew . . . friggin' flowers . . .

CHARLIE *moves away.*

CAROLINE *being interviewed.*

INTERVIEWER. Ms Giovanni has this tragedy affected the filming of *Quiet Valley*?

CAROLINE. As you can see most of the cast and crew are here to pay our last respects . . . so yes it has, but the people are so strong and resilient and have elected to continue filming this afternoon.

INTERVIEWER. Miss Giovanni. Did you know Sean Harkin . . .

CAROLINE. I didn't but from what I hear he was a well loved son and friend . . . we are all very shocked by the events. I just want to get my car please.

INTERVIEWER. I believe he wanted to be an extra on the movie.

CAROLINE. I wouldn't know about that . . . (*Walks away.*) Jock I'm ready.

INTERVIEWER *goes after her.*

INTERVIEWER. And what do you think of Ireland.

CAROLINE. Oh it is so magical . . . the country is so dramatic.

INTERVIEWER. And when can we expect to see *The Quiet Valley*?

CAROLINE. Next year I would imagine.

INTERVIEWER. Well the whole country will be looking forward to it and thank you Ms Giovanni . . . (*Turns front.*) Kevin Doherty for R. T. E. in County Kerry.

Marquee music.

SIMON. That's fine for level, thanks. Could we have everyone in the marquees, we have set up and we want to get the interiors done . . . it will be long and slow so be prepared.

CHARLIE. Be prepared that's me Simon. Dib dib I was in the Brownies.

JAKE. What is it with you Charlie eh . . . every time I say something that might need a bit of serious head stuff, you walk away.

CHARLIE. What are you on about?

JAKE. In the chapel . . . you walked away from me.

CHARLIE. Hayfever.

JAKE. No that's just another excuse not to take on the real world . . . you change the subject, tell a stupid joke . . . what is going on behind that bloody annoying cheerful chappie eh . . . you can't be Mr Clown all the time.

CHARLIE. What . . . who says I can't . . . oh you want me to be like Matt Talbot, batin' myself up, that would suit you would it?

JAKE. No . . . just want to know what makes you tick.

CHARLIE. None of your business.

JAKE. You have nothing in your life you are going nowhere and why is it doing my head in and not yours . . . what is going on, I need to know?

CHARLIE. Who says I am going nowhere . . . I have done somethin' . . . I have my script . . . I have something.

JAKE. Read your script . . . it is the biggest load of oul bollicks I have ever read in my life.

CHARLIE (*sits on the ground*). Bastard . . . why are you hurting me? I never do that to you . . . why are you doing this?

JAKE. Charlie, it's every bad film you have ever seen, no story, cardboard people . . . I suppose it's based on real life experience . . . is the Hero you the one that goes in search of the baddies and blows them away . . . like Sean? Wake up for Christ sake.

CHARLIE. And what, be like you, walkin' around hatin' everything, everybody, lookin' for reasons to blame the world.

JAKE. I don't need to look for reasons, I look round me and so should you.

CHARLIE. Sean again is it? You are trying to use that kid to try to justify your own miserable existence . . . you want it to be your fault, you want to be able to say that kid died because of me . . . no, believe me, you're not that fucking important.

JAKE. I could have gave him hope.

CHARLIE. You couldn't have give him nothing,

JAKE. I could!

CHARLIE. No you couldn't. It was too late.

JAKE. It wasn't.

CHARLIE. It was . . . I know I was where Sean was I woke up one morning and looked around me and I saw nothing . . . a big black hole of nothin' . . . and I wanted to jump into that big black hole as far down it as I could get, so I wouldn't have to wake up another morning . . . and when I woke up in the hospital, you know what I thought, my first thought . . . Charlie you are a pathetic bastard, you couldn't even do that right.

JAKE. Charlie . . . sorry . . . sorry mate.

CHARLIE. It's alright, it's just the day that's in it, the kid being buried, people are just over-emotional . . . ignore me . . .

JAKE. Charlie, sorry what I said about the film . . . I'll read it again.

CHARLIE. Nah, you are probably right . . . deep down I knew it was bollicks . . .

AISLING. Alright you two – into the marquee at once, less of the chit chat . . . the tables have been laid out as a banquet . . . I want no one touching the food until we have a take . . .

SIMON. Aisling, Aisling, get that drunken old bollicks off the set now. Clem is about to throw a wobbler . . . I said now . . . he has just knocked over a trestle table full of drinks . . . move him . . . (*On walkie talkie.*) Get me security. Why not. It's OK, I'll take care of it myself – OK you, you had your fun, now move.

MICKEY (*drunk*). they can't sack me I am in the can, Jake . . . they can't sack me, the last laugh is on me Mickey Riordain . . .

(*Sings.*) When all beside a vigil keep, the West asleep
The West asleep Alas and well my Aisling weep
When Connaught lies in slumber deep
There lakes and plain smile fair and free
Mid Rocks their guardian chivalry.

SIMON. For Christ sake . . . (*To* MICKEY.) Right you, you were warned . . . move it.

MICKEY. You can't sack me, I am in the can.

SIMON. There are three hundred and fifty of you in the can . . . nobody is even going to notice, now move it and don't come back.

MICKEY. You can't sack me . . . I am the only surviving extra on *The Quiet Man*, you can't sack me.

SIMON. Move or we will call the police.

MICKEY. You see this ground you are standing on ya jumped
up gobshite, this belonged to my Grandfather, and you are
telling me a Riordan to get off my land . . . what is
happening to the world Jake, what is happening to the
shaggin' world.

SIMON. Aisling call the guards will you, there is going to be
trouble. This oul bollicks won't leave.

MICKEY. No . . . there's no need, yous had young Sean
Harkin put out onto the street in his own town and you are
not going to do that to me.

JAKE. Don't go, Mickey stay . . . you never let nothing beat ya
Mickey, stay.

MICKEY. I will go of my own free will . . . in fact I resign.

Sing oh, let man learn liberty
From crashing wind and lashing sea.

Straightens himself . . . holds his head up.

CHARLIE. Jake . . . let him go, don't start. I can't take no more
of this . . . I am going into this marquee now, I am doing
what is asked of, I'm keeping my head down and that's that
so don't fucking start because I don't want to hear no more.

JAKE. Charlie wait.

CHARLIE. I said knock it on the head.

JAKE. No listen, remember what you said earlier when the
Director wasn't going to stop for the funeral, you said, sure
stick it in the film, this is the movies you can do what you
want . . . You are right Charlie, it's only a story . . . if it was
a story about a film being made and a young lad commits
suicide . . . in other words the stars become the extras and
the extras become the stars . . . so it becomes Sean's story,
and Mickey and all the people of this town.

CHARLIE. Yes and . . .

JAKE. Why couldn't it be done, don't we have the right to tell
our story, the way we want it.

CHARLIE. We could tell it 'til the cows come home but would that . . .

JAKE (*excited*). Yes cows . . . that's it . . . that's where it starts . . . Brilliant Charlie . . . the cows are where it starts and finishes . . . as he walked into the water to die the last thing he would have seen were the cows, the cows that should have been his future in the field looking at him . . . what do you say Charlie . . .

CHARLIE. What, you mean we do this movie?

JAKE. Why not, eh, we have just witnessed it all, haven't we . . . you have been where Sean was, you could get into his head better than anybody . . . you can write a script.

CHARLIE. A script . . . you told me it was a load o' bollicks.

JAKE. Yeah the story was, but you did it . . . you sat down and did it.

CHARLIE. Who is gonna listen to the likes of us?

JAKE. Well you must have thought somebody was gonna read your script. Otherwise why were you shuvin' it up everybody's nose?

CHARLIE. I knew they wouldn't . . . isn't that pathetic . . . I knew nobody would read it.

JAKE. You are full of shit man.

CHARLIE. You say that to me again and I will swing for you . . . Mister hate the world . . . I can't take any more knocks . . . do you hear . . . no more.

JAKE. Sorry Charlie, sorry, alright I understand . . . I do . . . Charlie it's just . . . how do I put this . . . Charlie, you and me are fucked, we have nothing, and we are going nowhere, but for the first time in my life I feel I can do something . . . they can only knock us if we don't believe in ourselves . . . and I believe this could work Charlie I do . . . Please give it a go, we have nothing to lose, no money no reputation, no assets.

CHARLIE (*indignant*). I have a tent.

JAKE. That's it. Canvas Productions.

CHARLIE. What?

JAKE. Thanks Charlie.

CHARLIE. Hey stall the ball there I never . . .

JAKE. We have the story, we go to one of these people here and say, tell us where to go from here . . . they all started somewhere.

CHARLIE. They're all too busy clawing their way up to the top to stop and listen to us.

JAKE. Tomorrow at breakfast we get yer man Clem the director . . . he sits over on his own and has his breakfast . . .

CHARLIE. Well, what do we say to him?

JAKE. Tonight we plan out our strategy in our Production Office.

CHARLIE. Wha?

JAKE. In the tent . . . Canvas Productions . . . float it on the Stock Market.

CHARLIE. Yeah and if it rains we will be floatin' with it.

CLEM *is munching his breakfast and thinking.*

JAKE. So the last image you see is Sean, going into the water and the cows watching him . . . the cows that should have been his future, watching him as he drowns.

JAKE. Well Clem, what do you think?

CLEM. It's just not sexy enough.

JAKE. What . . . what do ya mean?

CLEM. What if the Kid was pursued by Drug Pushers.

JAKE. But he wasn't.

CLEM. Movies aren't real life . . . excuse me for a second . . . (*He speaks into his walkie talkie.*) Aisling sweetheart could you bring me some more coffee . . . no sugar, watching the

figure . . . you're a gem . . . (*To* JAKE.) Where was I . . .
Oh yes . . . you are going to need a love interest.

JAKE. He loved the land . . . his cows.

CLEM (*winces*). Oh I've got a good idea, what if Fin was a
girl . . . the girlfriend who tried to keep him straight.

CHARLIE. But Fin was his mate, he was all Sean had, he
couldn't keep a relationship with a girl.

CLEM. Well I am only trying to tell you, you won't move it
unless you are aware of these elements . . . thank you
Aisling, you are an angel . . . are we set up for the first
shot?

AISLING. Almost there Clem.

CLEM. Good, give me a shout I won't be long . . . look boys
why don't you take it to the Irish Film Board?

JAKE. But this could happen to any kid, any rural kid.

CLEM. Sure, but it's not commercial enough. How many
people want to see a film about a suicide? People want
happy endings. Life is tough enough. People don't go to the
movies to get depressed.

CHARLIE. How can you have a happy ending about a kid who
drowns himself?

CLEM. He doesn't.

JAKE. But he did.

CLEM. No . . . the farmer who sees him walk into the water
actually saves him . . . just in time.

JAKE. And then what?

CLEM. Well . . . that's the end.

AISLING. We're ready for you now Clem.

CLEM. Super . . . must go . . . oh by the way do you have a
title for it?

JAKE. Yeah . . . *Stones in His Pockets*.

CLEM. What do you think of that Aisling, as a title for a movie.

AISLING. Doesn't say much . . . not very catchy . . . a bit nondescript.

CLEM. This girl is learning well . . . right Aisling let's move.

CHARLIE. First knock back . . . and Canvas Productions was only launched last night . . . that must be a record.

JAKE. Do you think they are right?

CHARLIE. No . . . No . . . Jake . . . I don't.

JAKE. Jesus . . . neither do I . . . god. All the time he was talking I kept saying to myself you are wrong . . . Charlie for the first time in my life I believed me.

CHARLIE. I'm so used to believing everything I do is bound to be no good.

JAKE. Not this time Charlie.

CHARLIE. No . . . not this time.

JAKE. So you have the opening scene of the the film, people comin' onto the land to ask Mr Harkin can they shoot over the landscape . . . but we see it from the kids' point of view and him a wee buck.

CHARLIE. So all you see is cows, every inch of screen, cows . . . cows, just cows and in the middle of it all these trendy designer trainers.

JAKE. Like Aisling's?

CHARLIE. Exactly, sinkin' into a a big mound of steaming cow clap . . . this is the first thing this child sees, the first intrusion into his world.

JAKE. Yeah . . . Cows . . . big slabbery dribblin' cows.

JAKE *and* CHARLIE . . . *animated.*

JAKE. Udders, tails, arses, in your face.

CHARLIE. Fartin', atin', dungin' . . . mooin'.

JAKE. Big dirty fat brutes . . . lukin' at ye . . . wide shots.

CHARLIE. Yes, mid shots.

JAKE. Yes. Close ups.

BOTH. Yes.

Blackout

The End.

A NIGHT IN NOVEMBER

A Night in November was first produced by DubbelJoint Productions at The West Belfast Festival, Whiterock, BIFHE, Belfast on 8 August 1994, then toured extensively throughout Ireland, and was also seen in New York. It was first staged in London at the Tricycle Theatre in March 1995 with the following cast :

KENNETH McCALLISTER   Dan Gordon

Director Pam Brighton
Design Robert Ballagh

ACT ONE

*The setting and props are minimal. The back drop is a
representation of a football crowd; the staging is a rostra
which has three levels representing the terrace.*

*The rostra is painted red, white and blue which flips to green,
white and orange when Kenneth reaches Dublin airport. The
only props are a World Cup T-shirt, shorts and hat. The actor
moves around the stage creating the environment and plays all
the characters without the aid of other props or additional
scenery. The actor creates sound effects when necessary.*

*As lights come up, Kenneth McCallister a minor civil servant
in his thirties, walks onto the stage. Further stage directions at
the discretion of the director.*

KENNETH. That day started out like every other day starts
   out . . . check under the car for explosive devices . . . you
   have to be a step ahead of them bastards . . . they keep
   advancing their technology, gone are the days of the good
   old fashioned learnt at their mother's knee trip wire attached
   to the ignition, now they can blow you up with a device no
   bigger than a box of matches . . . they'll not get me . . . then
   out she comes, I see her feet coming at me from where I'm
   lying under the car . . . advancing on me, like two great
   black patent rottweilers, I watch them as they come to rest
   just in my eyeline, I glare at them, they glare back, I take
   them on . . . look them straight in the eye and wait.

For dear sake Kenneth, who would want to blow you up?

I am a government employee.

You're only a dole clerk, Kenneth, will you catch yourself
on.

(*He mimics her.*) You're only a dole clerk Kenneth, only a
dole clerk, Kenneth, only a glorified charity worker, pen
pusher, not even a real dog, a bloody poodle or one of them

other skittery wee mongs that only shit in litter trays, not even a real dog, not even important enough to be on a hit list . . . bastards.

Daddy can I go with you and Granda Ernie to the football match?

NO . . .

Daddy can I go then?

NO . . .

If he's not takin' me he's not taking you, isn't that right Daddy?

No . . .

Then that means you're takin' me?

No . . .

But you said you weren't taking him if you're taking me which means you are taking me . . .

No, you're not going, I don't want to go, but I have to take Granda Sixty Cigarettes A Day Ernie because Granda Polluted Lungs can't go on his own and Mammy in her wisdom has instructed Daddy to take Granda Nicotine because Granda can't get up the steps on his own because he has inflicted early death on himself so thank you very much Mammy.

You don't like my father do you . . . ?

NO.

Jumps out of the car.

Ah, good morning, Box D and how are you . . .

Dead on Kenneth . . .

And what have we this morning, Box D?

A Fresh Claim Kenneth.

Aaggh Fresh Claims. I love Fresh Claims . . . love it love it love it love it.

Sits down.

. . . Next.

Fill that in . . . and sign there.

Where?

There.

Sorry, where . . . ?

There do you see where I have put that big gigantic X, that huge big black enormous X, that great big hulk of an X which I put there to make sure you sign in the right place . . . there, Patrick McCardle, Dependants . . . ?

Six.

Children?

Aye . . . fuck sake what else wud they be.

Six children?

Aye, wud have been seven but she lost one . . . you know.

Oh dear . . .

Available for work from today?

. . . Yes . . .

. . . Yes? . . .

Yes . . .

Good, you'll be wanting family income supplement, eh, I'll give you an appointment for . . . tomorrow a.m.

. . . Sure I'm here now . . .

So?

So can I not see them people now . . .

So am I . . .

So are you what?

Here now but I have to come back tomorrow don't I?

Aye, but I won't be here . . . I have to go to Dublin.

(*Writes.*) Not available for work as out of the country.

What . . . I'm only going to Dublin for the morning.

You're out of the country.

I'm going out on the eight o'clock and back on the eleven o'clock, I'm only taking my oul ma down to meet her sister who is meeting her at the station.

You're out of the country.

I'm not gettin' off the train I'll only be helping her onto the platform.

The train will be in a foreign country and you will be on it and technically speaking you are not available for work as you are out of the country.

Standing on a platform?

A foreign country platform.

I'm available for work until I get to Newry which will be about nine then on the way back I'll get to Newry about twelve. So, I'll only be out of the country for three hours . . . so if I tuk my lunch break, two tea breaks and two toilet breaks altogether and worked a half an hour overtime I could go to a foreign country and back and do a day's work so what's the problem sunshine . . .

Right, you want an appointment do you . . . for today, sir . . . that should be no problem if you would just like to take a seat and I shall call you at the first available appointment . . . you don't mind waiting sir . . . just over there. (*He watches him go.*) Just over there where I can watch you waiting and waiting and waiting you clever bastard. Sorted that one out Box D, didn't I . . .

You did Kenneth.

Trying to make a mug of me.

He was Kenneth.

We know how to sort the feckless hallions out, don't we
Box D?

We do Kenneth.

By my reckoning there won't be another appointment until
at least tomorrow, but I am going to enjoy you waiting Mr
Smart Ass . . . yes Audrey, I will have a cup of tea and two
jammy dodgers please . . . what . . . why not, he usually
takes custard creams, so he just decided to have one of the
only two remaining jammy dodgers because he knows I like
them, that's why . . . I'll remember that, and you tell him
Audrey that Kenneth Norman McCallister will remember
that . . . Next.

Lifts phone.

I told you before Debrah, don't phone me at work, Jerry
doesn't like it . . . what . . . what does it say . . . honest, I've
been accepted . . . no kidding Debrah . . . that's fantastic . . .
me, they have accepted me, I can't believe it . . . it's an
honour alright, they are all doctors and bank managers and
God knows what . . . what do you mean don't let you down,
what do you think I'm gonna do . . . we are all the same on
the golf course love . . . I'll bet you it was because at that
second interview I said Philip Morgan comes to our house
for dinner, wait until I tell Jerry Duffy, he has been trying to
get accepted for two years now . . . Jesus, I can't wait to see
his face . . . (*Whispers.*) It's because he's a Catholic but the
club can't admit that, but he knows and you and I know but
nobody can prove it . . . get off the phone love, I have to go
into his office and tell him . . . there's the laugh, he is the
supervisor and he can't get accepted . . . that's one up for
me, love, brilliant . . . see you later.

Puts the phone down.

Jerry, I just left those files on your desk I have dealt with
them like you asked . . . oh, by the way, fancy a game of
golf on Sunday?

Sunday is a tough day to get on the course if you're not a
member, Kenneth.

(*Out front.*) I have waited for years for this moment but I must act casual . . . I don't want him to feel inferior, now control yourself Kenneth, it's all in your stride . . . right . . . here goes . . .

Well actually Jerry, that should not be a problem because I have just been accepted as a member and as a member, you will be permitted as long as you're with me . . . I'll call you later to arrange the time.

I had to get out, had to go straight out, straight out to the toilet and laughed.

I couldn't bear to look back at the envy on his face, the years of gloatin', with that 'I got the post over a Protestant' look wiped off his face . . . because Jerry son, whether you like it or not, you'll never be one of us, at the end of the day, when the chips are down, when hardy comes to hardy, even when the fat lady sings we will always stick to our own . . . me a member of the Golf Club, him my boss and him having to kowtow to me to get on the course . . . things are looking up for Kenneth Norman McCallister . . . member of the Club.

Opens the car door and winds the window down.

Wind your window down Ernie would you please . . .

It's November.

I know it's November, Ernie, but you also know Ernie, November or not I don't allow smoking in the car and seeing as how you can't go five minutes without a cancer stick, Ernie, you will have to contend with the November winds . . . so you have two choices, freeze and smoke or be warm and stick a patch on . . .

I don't like football Ernie, so I hope you appreciate this.

Don't like football, you're not a man at all . . . I worry about you.

Do you Ernie, well did you know that your daughter is the wife of a man who has been accepted into the Golf Club, tell that to your cronies in the Buff Club.

Golf . . . that's an oul doll's game, the men in the Buffs
wouldn't be impressed by that, tell you what, you come
down with me and buy them a drink and that would impress
them, that's if they let ye over the door . . . they haven't
forgive me for lettin' my daughter marry a dole clerk . . .
I was called a traitor . . . I nearly think it wud have been
better if she'd married a Fenian, be more acceptable . . .
The scourge of Ulster is what yis are known by down in our
club. I have watched grown men reduced to wee childer by
yis . . . them men shouldn't have to beg for money of youse
clients, them is decent men who are out doing a day's work
to feed their childer.

If they are out doing a day's work then they shouldn't be
down at the dole, that's the problem.

(*Shouts out the window.*) . . . Go away back to your own
country.

What did you shout, Ernie?

That car that just passed has a Free State reg on it . . . Pope
lovers comin' up here.

So what, Ernie, they are up to see the match . . . support
their team.

Support a shower of half-baked Fenian lovers . . . I'd luk
over it if they were real Irish, but sure for Jesus sake the
half of them's English that weren't good enough to play for
England and then they discover some oul Irish bog woman
that was meant to be their granny, they never set fut in
Ireland before, wouldn't have known a shelalaigh from a
hole in the wall and now, be Jesus, you'd think they started
the 1916 Easter Rising.

Oh, so it would be alright if they were here supporting real
Irish.

No, it wouldn't but I'd luk over it.

Our Debrah was telling her Ma that now that you're a
member of the Golf Club, we can all go for a wee drink on
Sunday afternoons and take the kids . . . her Ma is all
chuffed, she has Freemans' club book out already pickin'

a frock, they are all doctors and bank managers and what have ye, says she . . . so I says to her, I'll be nice to a doctor when I'm sick and civil to a bank manager when I'm lukin' for a loan but when we are all drinking together I am as good as any man . . . aye drink is a great oul leveller. (*He spits.*)

It's 16 and 17 Ernie, they're over here.

Aye, we'll show the dirty Fenian bastards.

Aye, no surrender.

Is this a football match Ernie, or a crowd of lions waiting for the Christians . . . what's going on here.

They've got blood in their nostrils Kenny, Fenian blood, worse than that foreign Fenian blood and what's even more despicable than that, mercenary Fenian blood . . . here they come, here's our boys . . . (*Chants.*) Northern Ireland, Northern Ireland, come on lads show them Papish bastards how to play fut ball . . . luk, luk, there's Billy . . . (*Shouts.*) Billy Bingham for king. (*Sings.*) We love you Billy, we love you, so just tell them bastards where to go . . . that's our boys the Billy Boys, no problem . . .

Luk at them, luk at them dirty Fenian scum . . . BOO!

(*Ernie sings.*) God save our gracious Queen etc. etc.

(*During anthem.*) . . . Makes ye proud to be British when you hear that Kenny son, look our boys standing to attention, look at the Republic team, moving about, look at them moving about, make them stand still. . . make them . . . make them . . . look at them having to stand there, serves them right that they have to stand for ours and we are not playing theirs . . . serves them right because it is our country and them is all Fenian hallions . . . SEND HER VICTORIOUS . . .

Ernie, I must point out that that is the English national anthem and the ones who are not English live there anyway, so I am sure that it does not disturb them one way or the other and that all they want to do is play a game of football . . . well that was a red flag to a bull if ever there was one.

Oh, does it not, does it not, well let me tell you they may
luk like mere innocent futball players but as far as I am
concerned they are representing the I.R.A. get it . . . the
Irish Republican Army, understand, Republic of Ireland,
same thing, if they are prepared to sully themselves by
playing under the banner of the Republic of Ireland I don't
give a shite, if they are from Stoke on Trent or bloody
Blackpool because to me they are representing the men that
blow up our peelers or kill our soldiers . . . and what is
more, as far as the Protestant people of this province is
concerned, they are . . . Fenian scum.

Dirty Fenian scum . . . (*Chants.*) There's only one team in
Ireland.

Come on lads, get stuck into them dirty Taigs.

(*Starts to grunt.*) uh uh uh uh . . . come on boys kick the
ballicks off that big gorilla . . . where's your spear, you big
ape ye . . .

Ernie.

What's wrong with ye, sure they're fucking black aren't
they? . . . luk, three black men . . . (Shouts.) Hey, where did
you get your players . . . the zoo? (*Laughs.*)

Then all around me . . .

Trick or Treat, Trick or Treat, Trick or Treat, Trick or Tre . . .

Hear that Kenny, hear that, our boys miss nothin' . . .
(*Laughs, then shouts.*) Greysteel seven, Ireland nil . . . do
da do da . . . hey listen Kenny, listen . . . they're all at it
now, Greysteel seven, Ireland nil, do da do da day . . . hey,
I started that one and now thousands has joined in, it was
me that started it, me Ernie Thompson, magic.

Greysteel seven, Ireland nil, Greysteel seven, Ireland nil . . .

I felt sick, I felt such shame . . . ashamed of him, ashamed
that I'd married someone who came from him, ashamed of
standing in the same place as men like him . . . it's beyond
words, it's beyond feeling . . . I'm numb . . . Greysteel
seven Ireland nil . . . trick or treat . . . men walk into a pub

on Halloween, shout Trick or Treat and mow down seven
innocent people and these fuckin' barbarians are laughin' . . .
surely to God, surely to Christ these are not the people I am
part of . . . no, it's not, don't tell me, I'm not hearing them,
I'm not for I can't fucking handle it . . . Then I started.

Ernie, you are low life at its lowest, you are the foulest
human being that I have ever had the misfortune to know . . .
you know if you were dead I wish I could be the first
maggot to eat at your festered brain . . . the first worm to
bore into your stinking heart, the first dog to shite on your
grave and the last person to see you alive because then
I could say all this to you, but I can't Ernie, because
I look around me and there are hundreds of Ernies and
I am numb . . .

Then I could see a couple of men looking at me not
chantin' and I got scared so I started to open my mouth and
close it like I was saying what they were saying . . . then
I clocked the man beside me . . . I knew he was a Republic
supporter because he had his head buried hoping he
wouldn't he spotted not chantin' or cheering and I wanted to
say . . . me being nice to a Catholic for no good reason . . .
I wanted to say, luk, at me I'm only opening my mouth and
closing it, do what I'm doing and you will be alright, but
Ernie was getting over-excited, more obscene and God,
I wanted to grab the man beside me and run him out of the
place with my hands over his ears . . . then a goal . . . a goal
for Northern Ireland and the place erupts and the man beside
me stands up and claps desperate not to give himself away.

You're not going to the USA, doo da, doo da . . .

This is not a football match, it's a battle field, it's not about
who wins, it's about who doesn't win . . . please God, make
it a draw.

Dirty turncoat . . . luk at that Lundy . . . Lundy . . . Lundy . . .
That wee bugger was born here and now luk at him playing
for the Fenians . . . kick the wee bollick's shite in.

Get me home get me out of this . . . the crowd in front
started to sing the Sash and Ernie'd joined in with great
gusto, then a dig in the ribs from Ernie.

Join in, do you want the lads to think you're a half-baked
Prod or somethin' . . . sing.

And I sang, spitting the words out . . . spewing out the
words of a song that I grew up with that I'd sung with such
passion so many times and now the words and the tune
seemed so despicable.

And the Republic scores and there is a deathly silence apart
from the players who are not even sure they scored because
no-one is cheering . . . the Republic supporters desperate
not to give themselves away stand in silence hoping no-one
can detect any signs of pleasure on their faces, and the Billy
Boys are silenced for a moment as their cold eyes scour the
grounds looking for the one Irish supporter who can't
control his feelings, and the man beside me can't cheer or
clap he just looks blank hoping to God he has no signs of
joy on his face . . . frightened to clap he just stares straight
ahead, I look at him and he looks away . . . I nudge him and
whisper out of the side of my mouth 'Well done mate' . . .
I had this great rush of adrenalin when I said it . . . the man
didn't respond, probably thought, it's a trick they want me
to give myself away . . . of course he thought that, why
would he trust me in the company of Ernie, delirious with
hate.

And the Sash My Father Wore starts up again, just to show
the Billy Boys won't be silenced for long . . . and the crowd
of men in front look at the man beside me and I hear the
poor man beside me sing it, trying desperately to fight for
the words and I sing it in his ear, not to provoke him, but to
help him . . . he realises I am not his enemy and he trusts
me.

And then the final whistle . . . the man beside me rushed
away with his head down . . . desperate to escape as if he
had just committed a crime . . . I wanted to go after him . . .

Come on Ernie this way.

Houl on, houl on, no rush.

The game is over, come on.

You want people to think we are not proud of our boys . . . do you want to sneak off as if them dirty Pope lovers got the better of us . . . I'll tell you what, if I was a fitter man, the first smug lukin' Freestater I saw would be picking his Fenian teeth out of my boots . . . (*Shouts.*) Trick or Treat.

I drove home that night with the dreaded Ernie . . . I wanted to scream, wanted to stop the car and throw him out . . . but did I . . . no, I sat there and listened and hadn't the bottle to challenge him . . . no, too many years of accepting what Ernie accepted, so I sat in silence, knowing in my guts that Ernie had to be wrong, but Jesus Christ, where does that leave Kenneth Norman McCallister.

And as he took another gulp of air I prayed to God that it would be his last, but no fear.

You know what, Kenny, I don't care if them Fenians are gettin' to go to the World Cup, sure they'll get bate any-way . . . aye, let them go back to Ireland bummin' and blowing that they are going to America but as far as I am concerned we showed them . . . good night.

What can you say, what can you say to a man like Ernie, sixty-five years of good old loyal bigotry, sixty-five years of salt of the earth racism, and sixty-five years of being at the bottom of the heap, look at him, can hardly walk, hardly breathe, fifty years of smoking himself to death but tonight Ernie is a happy man, because tonight Ernie got the chance he has been waiting for all those years . . . to express himself . . . God help us all.

I turned on the car radio . . . I heard a player being interviewed after the match . . . an English man, born in England of an Irish mother telling the commentator as he stood in Windsor Park in Belfast that he was happy for all his fans back in Ireland . . . back in Ireland? . . . where did he think he was . . .

(*Gets out of the car.*) . . . She's waving at me out the window, she never waves at me out the window . . . she's been watchin' and waiting for me because tonight she is proud of me . . . tonight I am not only a dole clerk . . .

tonight I am a member of the Golf Club and at last she can up her status at aerobics.

Kenny, love, Valerie and Kyle say congratulations, Lisa and Malcolm want to buy you a drink and Pauline and Stuart pretended to be chuffed but I could sense as soon as I told Pauline that she was dead jealous . . . you'd know she was because as soon as I told her there was a few seconds silence, before she said Oh, Debrah, I am delighted for you. She was just the same when I told her Philip Morgan was coming to our house for dinner.

I have never witnessed such a despicable display of hatred as I have tonight.

I can imagine . . . anyway, wait 'til you hear this, Pauline is going to get her Mummy to knit you a sweater, you know the ones with golfers on and the best about it is she only knits those for ones that are actually members of clubs, she has this wee thing about only doing it for ones that are proper members.

They were shoutin' Trick or Treat, how can people stoop so low . . .

They are all scum, one side is as bad as the other, pay no heed to them . . . the kids don't mind that they can't get the new computer, I sat them down and said Daddy is a member of the Golf Club and it's a big thing . . .

Debrah, I am talking about your father, your father was ranting and raving like a man possessed with hatred, and . . . and . . . racism and . . . bigotry . . .

Don't mind my daddy, he always gets carried away at football matches . . . anyway, tell me what Jerry said . . . I bet he was livid, you got your own back, didn't you, let's have a glass of wine, we still have a bottle left over from last Christmas.

I cracked . . .

Listen you stupid empty-headed bitch, I don't want Jerry to be livid, do you know that, I don't want Jerry to feel like shit, I don't want him to go home to his wife and kids

knowing that I am out to get him for no other reason than
he is a Catholic . . . isn't that pathetic . . . but you don't
want your husband to be pathetic . . . you want your
husband to be a man and stand by his beliefs like your
disgusting father, you don't care about nothin' only me
wearing a stupid idiotic bloody sweater with a knitted golfer
hittin' a knitted golf ball with a knitted fucking golf club.

But I didn't . . . I said nothing because there are thousands
of Debrahs married to thousands of Kenneths and I hadn't
the balls to be the Kenneth that takes on the Debrah . . .
how could I blame her, how could I when I didn't even
know what I believed myself . . . I only knew that
something was happening to me, but how could I face it,
how could I stand there and look back at my whole life in
one night . . . instead I had a glass of wine with my wife
and tried to forget that awful night in November.

Ah, good morning Box D and what do we have today then?

The usual Kenneth.

Ah, the usual, how unusual.

Next.

You again . . . what happened, train strike?

No, you made me sit over there for two hours yesterday,
knowing I had to come back anyway . . . I'm sure you sleep
easy in your bed with the satisfaction of making people like
me feel like shit. I want to tell you something mate, I have
six kids, six kids and if I thought for one minute one of
them was going to grow up and treat another human being
the way you treated me yesterday, I would break their two
legs to make sure they never worked . . . now just get on
with it please because every minute I have to sit here and
watch you looking at me like I am some kind of scum, the
more I want to put my fist down your throat.

I had to get up, had to walk away . . . I looked into his eyes
and I saw the years of acceptance of people like me treating
him like dirt . . . years of accepting that he had to put up
with my pathetic bigotry . . . years of knowing that because

he was a Catholic, an out-of-work Catholic that he must accept being treated like he was nothing, of no worth and I looked into his eyes and I had to get up and walk away . . . he was right.

Excuse me would you, I'll get someone else to take over . . . sorry.

I stood in the middle of that office and looked round me. I watched myself sitting here for fifteen years, fifteen years of never looking into the eyes of anybody, thousands of faceless people with no eyes, no souls, no feelings, years of resentment and bitterness and pettiness and humiliation, just to make me, Kenneth McCallister a somebody. My head was spinning, I wanted to scream, wanted to jump up on the counter with a thousand giros in my hand and throw them at the people . . . here, go on, take the money, take the money and spend it on whatever you want, it doesn't matter, drink, horses, bingo, just go and have a good time on me . . . I watched myself do it . . . I felt I was standing there for hours just fantasising about what I could do if I wasn't a stupid little man, a stupid soul-less little prick . . . if it was even possible to change . . . was it . . . is it.

Audrey, I don't care if he ate the last jammy dodger the day again, you know that, I don't bloody care if he turns into a jammy dodger, just give me anything you have and I don't want tea today, I will have coffee, black coffee.

No, you're right, Jerry, I shouldn't have snapped at Audrey, I will go and apologise.

He turns to walk away.

I didn't know you liked football, Kenneth.

What, what did you say . . . what was that Jerry?

I saw you last night at the match but I was too far away to attract your attention. I never knew you liked football.

He looked at me, into my eyes . . . I felt like he had watched me commit a terrible crime . . . I'm sorry Jerry, I'm sorry, it wasn't me, you know that, it wasn't me, they don't speak for me, I was there and I was scared too, that's why

you saw me opening and closing my mouth, but I swear to
you Jerry, I said nothing, no Jerry don't think they speak for
me . . . oh, but they do speak for you Kenneth, think about
it Kenneth, think about the Golf Club Kenneth and you
throwing it in Jerry's face Kenneth, think about the bitterness you felt because Jerry got that job and he wasn't a
Prod, oh yes, Kenneth, they do speak for you, you're like
them, you're one of them, you've always been one of them,
so don't think that you can hide up in your nice semi and
get away with it, don't think because you are member of the
Club you can hide behind your hand-knit sweater and close
your ears to them, because you are part of them . . . you
can't escape so tell Jerry all that, go on, tell him . . .

I just had to take her Da . . . no interest myself . . . it was a
bit scary, like, a bit hostile, I did notice that.

We all expected that, Kenneth, we were prepared for that.

Were you, Jerry?

Oh, aye.

Were you scared, Jerry?

Well, I wasn't exactly laid back about it, but as I say, we
expected it . . . terrible pity, like, because it spoiled it for
the players, they couldn't perform so it spoils it for everybody . . . pity . . . awful shame.

(*Gets in the* car.) I drove home with Jerry's words pounding
in my brain . . . pity, he pities me, he pities me, who the
fuck does he think he is, how dare he pity us, him that was
trailed up in some Fenian gutter can sit there and pity me,
pity my people . . . I saw myself in Windsor Park . . . I went
back . . . I stood in the middle of the pitch and I shouted to
the hoards 'Shut up, shut up to fuck, they are not frightened
of you, they pity you, they are laughin' at ye, shut up, shut
up, don't let them laugh at you.'

. . . Trick or Treat . . .

Stop . . . stop . . . don't let them pity us . . . stop for fuck's
sake, stop . . . you're a joke . . . stop . . .

Kenneth, look at this, it says . . . Congratulations on your success, and inside the card it says . . . To Kenneth, well done, from Pauline and Stewart and she has even drawn a wee golfer on it . . . really nice of them, wasn't it . . . it probably galled them but it was still thoughtful.

I looked at my wife, I looked at her and I said to myself 'I don't love you, you have become a habit, like my jammy dodgers and my own special mug, we exist together.'

You fancy going out for a meal tonight Debrah, get a baby sitter, go for a meal and a bottle of wine.

Are you right in the head, Kenneth?

Yes and I fancy going out for a meal.

There is something wrong, Kenneth, what is it?

I want to take you for a meal tonight, you and me, just us.

You have lost your senses . . . A, it is a Tuesday night, B, we could not afford it and C, you know I am on a diet, so for God's sake, Kenneth, get a grip.

I hate it, I hate when she does her ABCs, nothing is a yes or a no or a maybe, everythin' has to have an A and a B and a C, never just an A or even an A and a B . . . always three . . . always, always.

For once can you not answer me with an ABC, just for once Debrah, just once do somethin' that shocks me.

Will you for God's sake keep your voice down . . . the children . . .

Look at me Debrah, look at your husband, your loyal boring predictable husband and tell me, tell me do you love me.

There is something wrong with you . . . have you been drinking?

No Debrah, I have been thinking, for the past ten years . . . we haven't thought about anything that's worth a damn to anybody . . . all you think about is you and all I think about is me, and what is really important to us is what other people think about us, and those same people don't give two

damns what we do or think because they are like us
thinking only about themselves . . . so what is the point . . .
what is the point, and if you say A, B or C, I will scream.

But she said nothing, she looked with desperate confusion
in her eyes, 'I've lost my husband' . . . that's the look the
poor girl had on her face, my husband is dead but he is
standing lookin' at me . . . I wanted to hug her and comfort
her and tell her it was alright. I looked at her sad little face
the tears in her eyes, I saw the wee girl with her dolls in the
pram dreaming of the white dress and the two children and
the semi and the good loyal husband 'til death do us part . . .
it didn't matter that she didn't love me really, Isobel doesn't
love Ernie, Ernie doesn't love Isobel, but they exist together,
why should I destroy all that for her.

She turned away from me, walked up the hall, lifted the
youngest and held him tight to her, the bigger one held her
hand.

Why are you crying Mammy?

(*Quietly*.) Daddy is cross with me.

Then she said nothing, just held onto them quietly weeping,
the eldest looked at me with his big sad accusing eyes and I
had to get out, get away, get away from those eyes . . . I
tried, but stopped and turned back.

Now, come on, Debrah, I'm sorry, go out into the garden
kids and leave me and your Mammy . . . I'm sorry, Love.

Did you mean all that Kenneth?

No, I don't know what has come over me, I'm sorry, forget
about it, forget I even said it . . . I'm just a bit pissed off
with work and I took it out on you, that's all.

You're sure?

Yes, love.

And she smiled, not believing me, but knowing for the sake
of her whole life, her whole existence that she must make
herself believe me. She will make herself believe with the
same will and determination that she does her step-ups in

aerobics, with the same rigour that she cleans the house, the same dedication she puts into making sure her kids are going to pass the eleven plus, the same will power she has for sacrifice to better herself because it is all part of the same thing . . . all part of the same thing.

We are the perfect Prods, we come in kits, we are standard regulation, we come from the one design, like those standard kitchens with the exact spaces for standard cookers and fridges, our dimensions never vary and that's the way we want it, but what happens when the kit is put together and the appliances don't fit the spaces . . . what happens . . . chaos, mayhem and we can't cope, we can't cope.

From that moment on, I knew I had to stop, stop before it was too late, stop before I destroyed my wife and our put-upable little life. No, to look back now could only mean total disaster . . . so Kenneth McCallister vowed that night that he would never look back again.

I had to train myself not to think, not to see, just keep your head down and get on with it . . . I didn't want to hear the news or think about who I was and where I came from and what I was supposed to think, I didn't want to listen to the men I'd voted for, the Unionist politicians spouting on and saying nothing only 'we won't budge, we won't change, we won't give in' . . . tried to imagine I was living in some insignificant little town in the middle of England, safe and surrounded and protected which was bearable until one night as I headed for the car after work . . .

Having problems with the car, Jerry?

Yeah, I'll go back in and ring a taxi.

I'll give you a lift home Jerry.

Why was I saying that, Jerry lived on the other side of town, bandit country, I'd never been there in my life, never had a desire to go there, but I was curious . . . I wanted to know beyond that man, where he lived, what his house looked like, what his wife looked like, what he had for his tea, what he thought about things . . . I couldn't ever imagine and for some daft reason I had to know, I wanted to know . . . I could hear the other Kenneth in my head, don't do it, don't do it, remember what you promised yourself, for the sake of your wife, your kids, your whole life, don't do it.

It's no problem, Jerry. Sure, she goes to aerobics and the kids are at their grannies on a Monday, so I've no need to rush home.

I drove up the Falls Road with Jerry, I had never been on the Falls Road in my life, never . . . the sun was shining, the road was hiving with black cabs and women and children and army tanks and normality and I was nervous, like a stranger in a foreign country, not sure of the territory, feeling like they were all looking at me, knowing I was a stranger, knowing I was the enemy but no-one paid a blind bit of notice, I fitted into the normality just like the soldiers . . . I felt a sudden rush of inexplicable anger . . . those soldiers look more at home here than me and this is my country . . . what was I saying . . . Jesus . . . then suddenly I began to laugh out loud.

If my wife could see me here now Jerry she would have a fit.

No kiddin'.

Never been up here in my life.

I've never been where you live in my life.

Funny, isn't it.

Yeah, weird.

And we drove in silence, what else could we say, funny, weird – that was what we said but what else could we say . . . two people who had worked together for fifteen years met on the golf course and yet two total strangers . . . funny, . . . yeah . . . weird.

Want to come in for a beer, Kenny?

I had pictured Jerry's house in my head, well, it couldn't be up to much I'd thought . . . he did live in West Belfast and we grew up with the pictures of deprivation and filth and

graffiti and too many kids and not enough soap . . . well, there it was, bigger than mine . . . detached with a garage, the lawn strewn with bikes and scooters and toy tractors, strewn with life, not like ours, manicured to the last blade . . . the unwritten rule BIKES AND SCOOTERS FORBIDDEN EXCEPT ON THE CONCRETE PROVIDED . . . grey cold concrete especially laid so the kids wouldn't ruin the grass . . . the grass was for show, concrete could be scrubbed afterwards . . . and inside Jerry's house was a whole other life, a life I've never known, a life of disorder . . . books upside down in the bookcase, not in order of size or colour . . . in our house only properly bound ones went on show . . . Debrah's order from the book club . . . burgundy leather bound classics . . . never opened, but they suit the bookshelf, match the wallpaper, blend in with the carpet, books that can't be allowed to vary just like the fitted kitchens. I once wanted to order a couple of Stephen King's from the book club, unbound . . . No, Kenneth, we are not spending all that money on something that has to be hidden away in a drawer and I accepted it, of course I accepted it, God help me . . . and there in Jerry's house, books of all shapes and sizes, books that looked read, had dog ears, piles and piles of them and I was jealous of Jerry and his disordered life and his higgledy-piggledy books.

'Fraid I can't offer you anything to eat, Kenny, I have to cook m'own the night, and I don't think that you would want to wait around while I burn it.

Wife not here, Jerry.

No, she's left a note on the kitchen table, she took a notion to take the kids to the pictures, so I'm to get my own.

Oh, God, what freedom, what wonderful unpredictability . . . and then at the bottom of the note which I strained my eyes to see, what Jerry never bothered to read out . . . Love You . . . why should he bother to read that out, it's a fact, it's unspoken, it's taken as read, but she still writes it, as a matter of course, just to make sure Jerry knows, but Jerry does know, so it doesn't matter if Jerry ever gets into the Golf Club because Jerry is loved by his wife, who still tells him . . . you lucky bastard, where did it all go wrong for me . . . where . . . how . . . why.

I drank the beer and left . . . I didn't want to go home, to be there when Debrah came in from aerobics . . . the woman I fell in love with had vanished into the perfect ten-by-ten square of our designed life, bound to the burgundy unopened classics and the scrubbed concrete . . . and me, her husband, the man she fell in love with tied to order and loyalty and nothing.

(*Young boy's voice.*) Hey, mister, are you from the Branch?

What?

Are you lookin' for touts or somethin'?

I had driven from Jerry's to East Belfast, the street where I was born, where I had lived until my mother and father could escape from the smell of poverty and people like themselves, striving for the day when they could move to a place where they could close their door on it all, saving for the day when they could get Venetian blinds so that no one could ever look in on their lives or judge them ever again . . . they could judge Jerry and his kind from behind the secrecy of the blinds . . . bikes and scooters scattered over the lawn meant slovenliness, a pile of jumbled up books meant no pride or dignity in their lives, a wife who said cook your own tea meant low life at its lowest and all this meant second class, filth, scum and hatred . . . and I believed it.

The kid had wheeled his bicycle right up to the driver's window and was leaning it and himself on the car and poking his wee face in at mine.

No, I'm not the Branch . . . I used to live in this street . . . No. 34.

If you're not the Branch, what are you doing round here . . .

. . . Do you live here?

Aye . . . over there . . . my Da was born in this street too you know, and so was his Ma.

What's your Da's name?

He's dead.

Sorry son.

My Da is a hero, he got killed trying to blow up a Fenian
pub . . . see, when I'm his age I won't get killed . . . I'm not
gonna miss, so I'm not.

What was your Da's name?

Norman Dawson . . . his photo's up on the wall of the
club . . . he's dead famous . . . have ye any money on ye
mister?

I gave him fifty pence and left . . . this time just driving
away, I wanted out into the country away from people and
their lives . . .

I had to think, I had to think about Norman Dawson . . .
dead famous.

I sat looking into the river, the Lagan and thought of
Norman Dawson. And I knew I couldn't go on pretending
that I lived in the middle of England.

The river was dark and slimy and I stared and stared trying
to see the bottom but years of silt and moss and pollution
made it impossible. Maybe at one time it was clear . . .
crystal clear, but never again.

Me and Norman were mates . . . Norman wanted to be a
soldier . . . join the army, he was obsessed by killing
Indians. I was always a sheriff, I enjoyed locking them up
and torturing them. Norman always wanted them dead. One
day they stopped being Indians and became Fenians, and
Norman stopped being a cowboy and became a UDA
commander in his Da's combat jacket . . . and I became a
Special Branch man in m' Da's sunglasses . . . and we
would play in Norman's house and his Da would laugh and
encourage us, 'how many Fenians did you kill the day,
Norman, son' . . . thousands, so I did . . . dead on, son . . .
I tortured them, Mr Dawson, so I did, I gave them some

shit, so I did . . . stop that bad talk or I'll tell yer Ma . . . alright, I gave them some gip and then I tortured them . . .

We used to camp in his Ma's back yard, two feet away from the outside toilet . . . We'd lie, side by side, I knew every freckle on his face, every blackhead on his nose, we'd count them when we were bored waiting for our prey . . . perhaps Norman was just waiting for the day when he could really have someone to kill . . . no . . . no he wasn't a freak, a nutter, no, his picture is on the wall of the club and all the other Norman Dawsons who do it and get away with it and are hailed and become heroes . . . was I saved from being Norman Dawson by moving away to respectability and a couple of exams and a job that Norman hadn't . . . but are we that different . . . we all believed the same as Norman, but we couldn't dirty our hands killing Fenians, we were civilised so we closed our eyes and our Venetians and let Norman Dawson . . . we let Norman Dawson do it for us. Oh, yes, we showed our disgust, tutted loudly and then scurried back in to the ten-by-ten and never thought of Norman Dawson or his victims ever again.

You're home late, Kenneth.

Yes, Debrah . . . I gave Jerry a lift home and I went in and had a few beers with him.

You did what?

You heard.

Are you wise, going away up there . . . what was his house like?

Big.

Big? How big, big as this.

Bigger.

Bigger? . . . Detached?

Yeah.

I wonder how they managed that . . . what was his wife like.

She wasn't in, took a notion to take the kids to the pictures and told Jerry to see to his own tea.

Typical . . . poor fella, I suppose he is used to that
behaviour.

Yeah, he is.

Disgustin', after the man does a day's work . . . was it tidy?

No.

You see, they manage to trail themselves out of the slums
and then when they do get nice houses they let them go to
wreck and ruin . . . is it any wonder, Kenneth?

Is what any wonder, Debrah?

Is it any wonder they don't deserve anything.

If you don't mind Debrah, I think I'll go and cut the lawn
before it gets dark.

I hated my wife . . . I hated her so much, because she had
echoed what I'd always thought, so I hated myself . . .
before that awful night in November I accepted myself, put
up with myself but what does a man do when he loathes
himself?

End of Act One.

ACT TWO

KENNETH. You wanted to see me Jerry.

I'm worried about you Kenny, you have been looking desperate this while back.

I'm alright, Jerry, honest.

You can talk to me.

Oh God, if only Jerry knew how much I wanted to talk to him but years of training on keeping yourself to yourself was a hard habit to break.

It's nothing Jerry . . . work gets you down sometimes, doesn't it.

Aye, sure, you'll be gettin' your holidays soon, going anywhere . . .

Debrah's mother's caravan in Ballybalbert, we go every year.

That'll be nice.

Going anywhere yourself, Jerry.

. . . America, and I can't wait, I'll tell you . . . counting the days.

America.

The World Cup . . . Ireland's playing, remember . . . they say there won't be an American accent to be found in New York the week of the matches . . . Jesus, it will be like the Pope's visit without the Pope . . . but then I'm sure Ballyhalbert is good crack too.

That will cost a packet.

My wife's sister is over in New York, so we'll have somewhere to stay.

Your wife's goin' too.

It was her idea, she's mad. I kept saying we can't afford
it, but she ignored me . . . Next thing I know she had the
kids organised to stay with her mother and the tickets are
booked . . . we were going to change the car but she just
said to hell with it, sure there is no crack in that.

Does your wife like football.

No, she can't stand it, she just wants to see Ireland winning,
she couldn't care less if it was bob sleighin' as long as
Ireland won and she was there to cheer them on . . . I mean
if you never liked futball the crack alone will be something
else . . .

Sounds great.

Anyway, cheer up, and remember I'm here if you need me,
Kenny.

Aye . . . and then out of the blue I asked him . . .

Jerry, why do you still live up there.

What?

You know, just wondering why you . . . you know . . . now,
I hope you don't think I'm too nosey but I was just . . . well,
it's been on my mind . . . the place is crawling with soldiers.

Why did I not buy myself out when I could . . . well, to be
honest, Kenny, I feel safe there and I'm not sure if I would
anywhere else . . . and I like the people, they're the ones I
grew up with, so I put up with the soldiers . . . I know it's
not ideal to go to work in the morning and trip over two
squaddies crouched in your driveway . . . and you see your
kids rushing past them munchin' away at their toast, but
sometimes I look into those scared eyes looking up at me
and sometimes I want to say 'Look, this is bloody
ridiculous, will you please come out from under my
rhododendrum bush, it is bright lilac and youse are dressed
in khaki, did youse learn nothing about camouflage', but
you know, they have been told that we are the enemy . . .
I thought I'd stop seeing them after a while, you know like

living beside a railway line you stop hearing the trains, but I
still see them . . . thank God.

Thank God?

Well, when I stop seeing them I suppose then I have
accepted them . . . here I shouldn't be talking like this . . .
I didn't mean to ramble on Kenny.

No it's alright Jerry . . . it's alright.

I went back to my desk and thought . . . yeah perhaps those
squaddies under the rhododendrons were . . . ridiculous . . .
how could I ever say that to anybody that I know? And then
I began to feel envious of Jerry having the freedom to
support Ireland, and I was jealous of that freedom – that he
had something he believed in – how could I say that to
anyone? I live in the same country and I am scared to
mention that I envy him . . . for me, it was dangerous talk,
for him, it's wild and wonderful crack . . .

I started to watch the news . . . I needed to know what was
happening . . . every night there was speculation on the
Downing Street Declaration . . . What was this . . . hope,
change, could it be, would it be . . . and then the hoover
would go on, she always puts the hoover on when politics
are mentioned . . .

The news is on, the floor isn't dirty.

She can't hear because the hoover is on.

Yes . . . it was like that when I was growing up . . . as soon
as the news came on my ma reached for the brush . . .
automatic reaction . . . don't listen . . . just keep cleaning
and everything will be alright . . . we have been protected
by hoovers and dusters and brushes all our lives . . .

Kenny, you are in another world, sitting there. Will you put
the nuts and crisps in a bowl, I have these vol-au-vents to
fill.

Ding, dong.

Oh, my God, Kenny and I'm not prepared, they're here . . .
I hate that, it's your fault, sitting there doing nothing and

I have to do everything and now look at the state of the place and me like a right mess.

Debrah, you are perfect, there is not one hair out of place, not one speck of dust that hasn't been exterminated, everything is shining, so what the hell are you talking about.

I still have my flipping slippers on, don't I?

Ding, dong.

Well, take them off for Christ sake.

And you are standing with crisp bags in your hand . . . and I know it's Stewart and Pauline and I know she will take all in that we are not even prepared and she will love it.

Then why for God's sake do we have bloody friends like Stewart and Pauline who judge us on whether we have managed to put six packets of cheese and onion crisps in bowls.

Just shut up and answer the door . . . and don't let her come into the kitchen.

(*Sarcasm.*) Welcome, do come in, sorry we are not prepared but do have a drink . . . Debrah is just adding the finishing touches to things, sorry we aren't ready, but I was engrossed in the news. Well, I haven't seen you since the Declaration. What do you think, Pauline?

What?

The Declaration that everybody is talking about . . . the Downing Street Declaration.

Don't talk to Pauline about politics, Kenny, she hasn't a clue.

I do have a clue, Stewart, I know they can declare all they want but at the end of the day it smacks of sell-out to me and our politicians will never allow that to happen so it's a pointless exercise . . . enough of all that . . . we are here to enjoy ourselves . . . I have a present for you Kenny . . . well, seeing as this is a little celebration not only for your birthday, but for you getting into the Golf Club, I thought

I'd mark it with these.

I wanted to laugh and scream at the same time . . . there they were, before my eyes, I held them and looked at them speechless . . . a set of knitted golf club covers with pom-poms on . . . red, white and blue knitted golf club helmets to keep my golf clubs warm, finished off with perfect little rounded fringed pom-poms, each little fringe exactly the same as the next . . . thousands of them . . . these must have taken up Pauline's mother's whole day.

Terrific, Pauline, condoms for my golf clubs . . . thank you, I am delighted about that, I was a bit worried about my eight iron and my putter. They were getting a bit close for comfort out on that green . . . I says right you two, no 'anky panky, unless it's safe sex, I don't want no wee putters running about.

She was not all that amused . . . Stewart was, he likes a dirty joke. He pulled me aside to tell me another one – Did you hear the one about the two nuns in the bath, one says wares the soap and the other says it does, doesn't it.

Out of the side of my eye, I see Pauline dart into the kitchen to wallow in my wife's unforgivable crime of failing to fill the vol-au-vents with mushrooms before eight o'clock . . . so I thought, tonight Kenneth, you may as well be hung for a sheep as a mushroom.

Ding dong, ding dong, ding dong.

Welcome, everybody, glad you could all come and help me celebrate thirty-four years of being an asshole but then I am in the right company.

. . . Laughs all round . . . they don't think I'm serious.

I . . . would like to ask you if any of you were embarrassed by the football match that took place between Northern Ireland and the Republic of Ireland . . .

Confused looks all round . . .

No, you probably did not take it under your notice, of course you didn't. Why should any of us be interested or

concerned that Ireland are through to the World Cup . . .
well, most of us here aren't really into football.

More laughs, this time polite, but slightly nervous.

Well, let me tell you what you missed. I know it was a few
months ago but you see it was one of those nights that is
hard to forget.

Debrah's vol-au-vent is stopped in mid-air.

We are all respectable people here in this room and I am
sure that if you had witnessed what I witnessed, heard what
I heard, you would be as ashamed as me . . . of course you
would.

No one is laughing now, dry embarrassed coughs, shuffling
from foot to foot, hands reaching for crisps in an attempt to
appear casual . . . a crisp falls on the floor . . . Debrah
clocks it, but puts it to the back of her mind.

Yes, you would all have tut-tutted at this disgusting and
ugly display of bigotry . . . you might even have been a bit
embarrassed . . . but were you ashamed . . . I don't think
so . . . is that because we can ignore those nasty low-lifes as
not being part of us, yet we vote for the people who feed
this evil. So why throw our hands up in horror when we
hear of another loyalist murder committed by the men who
fight and kill for Ulster, don't we all share Lord Carson's
legacy don't we all still believe that this is ours, this our
state and we must never give an inch. Don't they believe
like us that we must keep those dirty Fenians down? Yes,
it's alright not to employ them, alright to keep them out of
the golf clubs, alright to screw up their benefits, but if you
don't have the luxury of discriminating nicely and cleanly
then what do you do, eh? . . . What do you do if you are a
nobody and you still want to be part of Carson's army . . .
you do what my friend Norman Dawson did, wipe them out
in the only way you know how . . . why are you all looking
so horrified . . . horrified at the thought that you might he
classed as an ugly blood-thirsty barbarian. They are
carrying out Carson's orders, they are defending the legacy,
a legacy that left them nothing, defending it for us, so we

can sit back and enjoy it . . . so at least have the decency to
support them. If you don't, then for Christ's sake, come out
and have the balls to condemn them . . . and condemn, not
just what they do, but why they do it.

The silence was unbearable. I was aware of a pair of eyes
boring through me, hard eyes that froze me to the spot. I felt
I was jammed in the pupils, that if they blinked, I'd be
pulverised . . . it was Pauline.

You are British and you should be ashamed of yourself.

Pauline, you are dead fucking right . . . I am.

Needless to say, after that terrible night in April, we had few
phone calls from our friends. The word travelled fast that
Kenneth had lost his marbles and was being brainwashed
by Catholic workers in the D.H.S.S. . . . I still checked
under my car every day, but now I was scared of my own
people . . . Debrah and I barely spoke, well, what do
strangers say to each other . . . I suppose they find something, the weather, the price of beer etc. but those things
seem ridiculous if the strangers are living in the same
house, sharing the same bed and the same children. I'd gone
too far, said too much. I should be ashamed of myself –
I am British. So here I am on the island of Ireland being
told to be ashamed for questioning our right to hate.

It's like we're living at the top of a bloody great big house
and we think that we've got the best room, so we keep
ourselves locked in, and we won't even open the door to let
in fresh air. The air in the room is stale and we breathe it
decade after decade, year after year, day after day and we
are safe in our stale air.

Your Golf Club fees are due, Kenneth, don't forget.

This was how we continued our lives, we spoke when
necessary, fed each other relevant information, talked a lot
to the kids to cover silences . . . and at night, the unspoken
rule of whoever goes to bed first, wait until the other is
asleep before entering . . . that way it was bearable . . . this
wasn't just a normal marital argument that could be patched

up in a day or two when the heat died down . . . no, this did not need a patch, it was beyond patching, it was rendered obsolete, but we could not bear to deal with it.

Jerry was full of chat, one day at work.

Only a fortnight to go Kenneth . . . New York, here we come, Ole, Ole, Ole.

Yeah, sounds great crack, Jerry.

Twenty Aer Lingus flights leaving Dublin . . . they say there will be more people leaving Ireland that day, than did during the famine . . . I can't wait . . . be one big party from start to finish.

What if they don't win.

Since when would that stop us partying . . . the attitude will be, we didn't win, and we should have, so let's have a party to celebrate the fact that we could have, if we hadn't lost . . . know what I mean . . .

I wish Jerry wouldn't go on about America, I can't bear it.

Your Golf Club fees are a week late Kenneth.

Yes, Debrah, I am going to pay them soon.

I don't see why you left it so late, it's not as if the money is not there in the bank.

I do get one month to pay from the time of the invoice.

Yes, but I don't want them to think we have no money . . . or that we had to borrow it.

I am sure the accountant is not sitting thinking to himself, Kenneth must be in difficulties, oh dear, perhaps it was a bad idea to accept Kenneth as it is obvious he is not of the financial standing to be part of us . . . Debrah, don't you know, did anybody ever tell you that people with money have it because they hang onto it as long as possible.

Just pay it Kenneth, because I won't relax until you do.

Right, right, I'll go, I'll go and do it right now.

I drove past the Golf Club, in fact I drove past it five times and on the fifth time I drove home. Debrah was at aerobics, the kids were at their grannies. This gave me peace to work it all out, to work out the most exciting, totally outrageous crazy mad thing I had ever done in my life . . . 300 pounds I had for the half-year golf fees, one hundred pounds worth of electricity shares that my mother had bought me for my birthday, they could be worth 200 now . . . not enough . . . Christ, there must be something I could sell . . . the golf clubs must be worth at least 200 quid, I knew somebody in work who was looking to buy some . . . that would be enough, that would be just enough.

Every morning I woke up, I lay for five minutes asking myself 'Are you sure, Kenneth, now, are you absolutely sure you know what you are doing', and the answer was always the same . . . too bloody right I do, in fact I can't wait.

Everything worked out so smoothly, no hitches.

. . . I sold the golf clubs and I threw in the bag and the trolley that Isobel and Ernie had bought and I got £300 . . . and the electricity shares were wee buns and nobody knew a thing . . . it was then I knew what I was doing was destined.

The night before I could barely contain myself. I must not show any signs of unusual behaviour . . . I would fake falling asleep on the settee and Debrah would, as usual, leave me there and go to bed . . . but tonight, I was not asleep . . . I'd left work at lunch time and packed a small suitcase which I had hidden in the boot . . . I sat there watching the clock in the silence and never for one minute had doubts about what I was going to do . . . at six o'clock exactly I slipped quietly out of the house and into the car . . . as I was driving I felt I was like a car with no brakes speeding along, not to disaster . . . I was that car in Chitty Chitty Bang Bang when it came to the edge of the cliff, it took wings . . . that was me.

I crossed the Border for the first time in my life. It just never occurred to me to do it, we were taught to be afraid, to be afraid of the black magic, the dark evil, the mysterious jiggery Popery that'll brainwash us. But is that what it is? Is

that what our leaders are really scared of, or is it that if the
tables are turned they are afraid that we'll be treated the
way we've treated the Taigs and we'll be the second-class
citizens.

Yes, that could be part of it too, the fear of retribution –
they say they are God-fearing men. What they fear is their
own judgment day, their own behaviour staring them in the
face.

Dublin airport, 10 kilometres, yes . . . (*Starts to sing to
himself.*) . . . Trailer for Sale or Rent, Room to Let 50 Cents,
No Phone No Pool No Pets, Ain't Got No Cigarettes . . .
etc . . . etc . . .

I drove into the car park . . . it was a sight I'll never forget . . .
the whole airport had been taken over by a green, white
and gold army . . . there were check-ins going on in the car
park . . . people were singing . . . at nine o'clock in the
morning, they were singing and laughing and chanting 'Ole,
we're on our way, we're on our way to the USA.'

So am I, I shouted . . . I am going to New York, hey, me too.
I'm off to support Ireland in the World Cup, brill, isn't it,
lads . . . I loved saying lads . . . like I was a comrade . . .
like I was one of them . . . me and the lads . . . alright lads,
eh . . . Italy, no problem . . . Ole Ole Ole.

I had forgotten myself, I was jumping up and down like a
kid . . . a couple of lads started to laugh at my outburst, not
in a mocking way . . . just as though they understood . . .
yes everybody had a right to be happy that morning, everybody had their own story of how they got to be there . . . but
at this moment in time, we were all the lads . . . and it felt
good . . . people with streamers and hats and silly wigs and
painted faces and I was part of them . . . Oh, if only Pauline
could see me now.

Then I looked at myself . . . there I was standing out in
the thousands like a sore thumb. I was dressed like this,
God I looked like a right plonker . . . I looked more like the
airport security . . . maybe that was why they were laughing
at me . . . there was one man who was just standing smiling

to himself . . . he was fifty if he was a day . . . had a look of respectability about him, he looked as uncomfortable in his World Cup T-shirt and his shorts and silly hat as I did in my Dunnes menswear gear . . . but like me he had the look of a man who was about to be set free . . . we clocked each other and smiled.

Hey, mate, where do you get them T-shirts from.

What, the whole country is swamped with them, where have you been?

I've come from Belfast.

Oh, that's different.

He pulled the zip of his bag open and fumbled around and threw a T-shirt at me.

Here, for God's sake, put this on, you look like the man from the Welfare.

I laughed . . . I was, that's exactly who I was, but I wasn't telling him that.

Thanks mate . . . (*Puts on the T-shirt.*) How much do I owe you.

You can buy me a drink if I bump into you in New York.

I stripped off my shirt and tie and blazer, right there in the car park and put on the T-shirt . . . me standing in a green, white and orange shirt with a tricolour on it . . . unbelievable . . . unbelievable.

Myself and the man who give me the T-shirt made our way with the crowds to the terminal building.

Jasis, isn't this the business . . . isn't this what life is all about eh . . . would you look at us all . . . I tell you what, there is more borrowed money here than it took to crash Wall Street . . . ah, sure, if I hadn't done this I would regret it the rest of me life . . . much did you pay for your match ticket.

Oh, that, I haven't got that, sure I'll get it when I get there.

Are ye crazy or what . . . they will be selling at hundreds of dollars now . . . you have no chance.

Really . . . now I feel like a double plonker.

Tell you what, if we get split up I'll meet you in Eamon Doran's bar tonight on Second Avenue, I'm meetin' up with a few of the lads and we'll see what we can do, but I won't promise nothing . . . where are you stayin'?

What . . . am . . . Oh God, I didn't think about that.

You're well organised, aren't you . . . lukin' like the rent man, no match tickets and nowhere to stay . . . what were you thinkin' of.

I got here and I'm going to America and I never thought further than that.

Yeah I know what you mean . . . You know two days ago I was sitting in me office looking out the window at the rain. There was me trussed up in me suit and tie, surrounded by other robots in suits and ties, and I looked out me window at a travel agents across the street. I see two lads kitted out in the team colours, and they bounced out waving their tickets and singing and cavorting. And I said to meself . . . excuse the language . . . but I said to meself, fuck it. I got up, lifted my briefcase and walked out the door. I said to my secretary 'I'll see you when I see you, I'm off to America to watch Ireland winning the World Cup' and here I am, on my way to the USA.

Me too, that's what I did. I just said fuck it too.

The name is Mick, meet me tonight in Eamon's and I'll see if I can get you a floor to crash on . . . It's great I haven't crashed on a floor since I was a student and do you know what . . . I'm lookin' forward to it.

Me too . . . by the way, I'm Kenneth.

No problem Kenneth.

Dead on, Mick . . . thanks, mate.

As I walked across the tarmac, my feet were not even touching the ground . . . don't look back, Kenneth, you've got this far, once you're on that jumbo, you can't get off, you are there, don't have no last minute twangs of conscience, just one and you're sunk. As I walked towards the flight I knew it could go either way, so I said leave it to fate, Kenneth, just leave it to the gods and see what happens when you reach the last step . . . let them decide, because at this point in time you are not of sound mind, you have no responsibility for yourself and I loved it . . . I reached the top, the attendant said good morning. I stopped, looked back, the fella behind me moved slightly, as if to let me wave to my loved ones in the viewing gallery . . . I looked, I was about to head down the gangway . . . and fate and the gods must have said to themselves . . . fuck it . . . and I burst out laughing and waved, then turned away into the unknown . . . I knew then that there was no turning back now for Kenneth Norman McCallister, for now I really was one of the lads.

The wife . . . ?

It was the fella behind me . . . 'Sorry' . . . I was still sniggering.

Waving to the wife?

No . . . just someone I knew . . . Kenneth, his name is.

My wife thinks I've gone to Lough Derg . . . but I have me face paints and a wig in case I'm caught by the cameras . . . bleeding RTE are everywhere.

Another pipes up.

I told my wife I was going fishing in Donegal. I told the bank manager I was building a garage and I told my boss in work I was going to Granny's funeral . . . So, when I come back I'd better have a couple of trout, build a garage and kill me Granny.

I'm alright, nobody will see me, we don't get RTE in Belfast, or at least not where I come from.

Yeah, you're like me, if Ireland win this match on Saturday
I have to come home and pretend I'm not over the bleeding
moon.

Do you live in Belfast too?

No, I work for a bleeding Italian restaurant.

A lad who sat beside me was well gone, he had almost
demolished the contents of the duty free.

Were you at that match in Windsor Park?

I was.

I tell you what mate . . . he was speaking as he was trying
to put his seat belt on to the other half of mine.

Ah, that's my seat belt.

He ignored me . . . you see you Belfast men, I am proud
of yis, I am proud of the way, yis stood at Windsor Park
and took what yis had to take and yis stood there . . . I
didn't go . . . me . . . I was a coward . . . but I have to hand
it to you . . . here, take a slug of that whiskey, because
youse deserve a medal and Jackie's Army are proud of
yis . . . (*Sings.*) We're all part of Jackie's Army . . .

No you wouldn't have been proud of me, you see, I'm a
Protestant.

So am I.

Jesus, so he was . . . so he was and yet he said . . . God . . .
you lucky bugger . . . so was he and yet . . . ah, what the
hell . . .

Sure at the end of the day we are all part of Jackie's Army.

I took a slug of his whiskey and felt part of Jackie's Army
too.

Then he sat staring at me.

Something wrong?

Something wrong? . . . Are you drinking that whiskey or
makin' love to it.

Oh, yeah, thanks.

The flight across the Atlantic with Jackie's Army was
something I could only ever have dreamed of. We sang and
drank and carried on like we had been told these are your
last hours on this planet . . . Everybody was part of Jackie's
Army, the crew, the cock pit crew, the pilot . . . we were all
the lads . . . Irish lads on our way to support our team . . .
even the pilot was startin' the singsongs over the tannoy . . .
the lad beside me wanted to send him up a drink but we had
to draw the line somewhere. As the plane touched down in
JFK there was an almighty roar of Ole Ole Ole . . . oh God,
I was so deliriously happy . . . for a brief moment, I
checked into my own head to see if there were any feelings
of guilt or remorse or regret and I couldn't find one . . .
I even thought because I couldn't find one like that then
I should find thoughts of concern that I was selfish and
heartless . . . but no . . . I knew I was on a road that had
no turn-offs or roundabouts or even parking lay-bys . . .
no, I must go until the end, what happens after that, who
knows . . . and as I held onto the lad beside me, while me
and his mate carried him off the plane . . . he was so drunk
he couldn't remember the second line of Ole Ole Ole . . . as
we carried him off I looked at him and thought, you're right
mate, who cares, because however awful it is when I get to
the end of it, I will always have the wonderful memory of
being one of the lads (*Arms up in the air.*) Oh, sorry mate.

I'm in New York . . . I am in New York . . . I kept saying it
over and over to myself . . . it's just like the TV . . . I felt
part of a film set . . . yellow cabs, noise, Manhattan,
millions all talking at once . . . I took a cab to Eamon
Doran's bar to meet Mick . . . I didn't doubt for one minute
that he wouldn't turn up . . . I was one of the lads and the lads
all looked out for each other, I knew that instinctively . . .
after thirty-four years of looking out for yourself, it was a
lovely warm feeling of belongin'. This bar was just a
continuation of the flight . . . wall to wall Irish men in
green, white and gold still singing Ole, Ole, Ole . . . even
the pilot was there . . . it looked like total chaos and
mayhem . . . people making phone calls from numbers they

were given back in Ireland, somebody vaguely knew
someone who might have floor space.

Hello, I'm saying hello, my name's Kevin, you know my
cousin Robbie Hagan, don't you . . . no, you do . . . yes,
sure you grew up together before you emigrated . . . in
Cavan, yes . . . yes, I know it was 35 years ago. I know you
were only five, but he said that you said that if he was ever
in America to look you up . . . well, he's not here, so he said
for me to phone you and see if you have a floor I could
crash on, seeing as I'm here instead of him and I'm his
cousin and you know him and I'm from Cavan too . . .
terrific mate . . . I have a mate . . . great, hey . . . there's a
boy here with space for two more.

It was as if all these people knew each other . . . I suppose
this must go back to the Famine. Irish people landing here
and herded into sheds and then sent out into the unknown to
fend for themselves . . . I suppose from that day on it was
the unspoken rule that the Irish would have to look after
their own . . . even me, even me who never considered
himself an Irishman . . . in their eyes I was one of them . . .
and I loved it.

Kenny . . . Kenny.

It was Mick.

He looked twenty years younger than he looked in Dublin
airport, his silly hat and shorts and T-shirt now seemed
absolutely right and he knew it.

Here, take this address and number, you have floor space for
as long as you like . . . no luck with the tickets, but sure
some of the lads were saying you'd be as well off watching
it here, for the stadium will be like a chip pan, sure the
crack will be mighty.

That'll suit me Mick . . . and thank you very much for
everything you've done for me . . . as soon as I said it, I
knew it sounded like a line from a Helen Steiner Rice get
well card . . . but what the hell.

Well, me and Mick and some of the lads partied to the wee
small hours in Eamon Doran's bar . . . every now and then

I would nip down to the loo, look in the mirror to see if it was me . . . (*Reads his T-shirt in the mirror.*) elo, elo, elo, elo . . . laugh, then take the stairs four at a time back to my fellow Irishmen at the bar.

. . . And from that day on he always kept the chickens in the loft . . .

The next day – the day of the match against Italy, the temperature was 98 degrees in the shade.

(*Sings as he changes into World Cup gear.*) We're all part of Jackie's Army, we're going to the USA and we'll really shake them up, when we win the World Cup, cause Ireland are the greatest football team.

The atmosphere in Eamon Doran's was bloody electric . . . the bar was jammed with men and women . . . buzzin' with the kind of excitement I hadn't felt since I was a kid . . . and the women . . . just as knowledgeable about their team as the men . . . now, that did surprise me . . . I mean, women and football . . .

On your own, handsome?

Me.

Aye, you . . . standing there like the Tom that got the cat.

You mean cream . . . Oh no, what a stupid thing to say.

What?

You mean like the cat that got the cream . . . Oh Kenneth, just shut up.

What fecking use is a bowl of cream when you're dying for a shag.

What?

Ah, sure I'm only slaggin' . . . want to join us . . . we're over here.

I looked over and there was at least ten of them . . . God . . . me and all those women . . . am . . . oh God . . . I was scared . . .

Come on, we won't ate ye . . . well, not unless you're desperate . . .

What's your name?

Kenneth.

Girls, this is Kenneth, he prefers ating ice cream to shaggin'.

Dirty laughs all round . . . I can see I'm not going to come out of this one alive.

Packie Bonner, I want to have your babies.

It was a man said that.

The team were on the pitch.

Kenneth reacts as he hears the Irish National Anthem sung by everyone in the pub . . . He eventually rises, at first nervously and then defiantly.

(*Girls' voices.*) I don't think Andy Townsend should have tipped his hair . . . he doesn't suit it.

You should talk, look at that temperature, it must be 120 degrees out there. It's not fair, our lads have to play in that and look at them Italians all dead cocky because they're used to it, I hope you all get sunburnt.

Come on lads (*Sings as girls.*) We love you boys in green, we love you boys in green . . . sing Kenneth.

I don't know it.

Jasis, there's only one fecking line.

They sang it in my ear . . . each song in turn to teach me . . . to help me to be a part of them . . . I remembered that night in Windsor Park when I sang the Sash into that man's ear, so he could be part of us . . . to be part of us, so he could be safe from us . . . And then suddenly a deafening roar and I'm grabbed by at least six of the women.

What, what happened . . . A goal.

Jesus, we scored . . .

(*Sings.*) Stick your pizzas up your arse . . . come on Kenneth.

I don't know it.

Join in the chorus.

Stick your pizzas up your arse.

Why do all the songs have one line.

So, they're easy to remember when you're drunk.

The man who wanted to have Packie's babies now wanted to have Ray Houghton's, he was delirious.

God, I wouldn't have missed this for the world.

Come on lads. The second half started and Ireland were still ahead . . .

Oh . . . No . . . Ah . . . get back . . . oh . . . ah . . . oo ah Paul McGrath

And I wanted to have Paul McGrath's babies.

And then . . . and then . . . and then . . . the final whistle.

Kenneth is delirious.

We all piled onto Second Avenue and stopped the traffic . . . everyone just standing in the middle of the road . . . as the horns tooted and the traffic came to a standstill . . . nothing barrin' an earthquake stops traffic in America but we did, with our one-line songs . . . that's all it took . . . there were lads sitting on bonnets of cars . . . just singing and cheering and oblivious to the chaos it was causing . . . no tonight on Second Avenue, New York, it was our night.

I thought back to Windsor Park . . . I thought of those angry men and their Trick or Treat and their cold staring eyes and their hard bitter faces and I thought to myself Jerry was right . . . what a pity, what a shame that they can't allow themselves to be a part of this . . . what a terrible pity.

At one stage the police were called . . . expecting to find crazed drunken Irishmen about to wreck all around them . . . oh yes, they had heard of these wild untamable mad men and they came prepared, batons at the ready, armoured vans sitting in waiting . . . what a shock for these poor men and women of the NYPD.

Look out boys, it's the peelers.

Move to the sidewalk, immediately.

No problem, officer. Say officer, could me and some of the lads have our photographs taken with you. You see no-one is going to believe we were in America and we couldn't be arsed to go all the way to the Statue of Liberty.

Sure just give me a minu . . .

Great lads, he says, it's okay, everybody back.

No, I didn't mean . . .

You're a smasher, you are, you're just like that big fella in the Miami Vice, isn't he, smile . . . (*Sings.*) We love you boys in blue, we love you boys in blue – God, we loved beating the Italians.

I was singing at the top of my voice . . . 'Stick your pizzas up your arse' . . . everybody took it in good stead, even the Italian policeman . . . well, almost . . . I stopped to get my breath and a drink when this policeman came over to me.

Where are you from in Ireland?

Me . . . Belfast . . . I am an Irishman from Belfast . . . I was enjoying saying that.

It's just been on the news, there was a dreadful shooting near Belfast tonight.

What . . . where . . .

Some guys were watching the match when a couple of gunmen came in and shot dead six of them . . .

I watched this wild and wonderful harmless celebration of human beings just simply bringing out the best in themselves . . . just a parade of the best there is in human nature and tried to connect it with the worst . . . impossible . . . just impossible.

What's up with ye mate.

It was Mick, back from the match and as happy as I'd ever seen a person.

I told him what had happened back home.

He put his arm around my shoulder and pulled me into him . . . another man has never done that to me, but it was right for Mick to do it . . . he knew what I felt. Mick and I had shared something, we had both said Fuck It in our lives and we were mates.

Come on in and have a drink Mick . . . I want you to drink with me, because tonight I can stand here and tell you that I am no part of the men who did that . . . I am not of them any more . . . no, no-one can point the finger at Kenneth Norman McCallister and say, these people are part of you . . . tonight I absolve myself . . . I am free of them Mick . . . I am free of it, I am a free man . . . I am a Protestant Man, I'm an Irish Man.

The End.